With Bible in One Hand and Newspaper in the Other

With Bible in One Hand and Newspaper in the Other

The Bible in the Public Square

Charles R. Peterson

RESOURCE *Publications* · Eugene, Oregon

To Barb

He has told you, O mortal, what is good;

and what does the Lord require of you

but to do justice, and to love kindness,

and to walk humbly with your God?

MICAH 6:8 (NRSV)

Contents

Preface

IN 2009, SOME LETTERS to the editor of the (Minnesota) *Brainerd Dispatch* criticized the debate and process that welcomed homosexual persons into the Evangelical Lutheran Church of America (ELCA). Not long before, we had retired to our home near Brainerd, Minnesota, and I wrote some letters to the Dispatch editor in response to provide what I regarded as a more accurate perspective. This began a series of opinions on broader issues.

A couple of years later a new and politically conservative editor and I had some conversations that resulted in an unsolicited invitation for me to serve a term as community representative on the editorial board. My role was to meet weekly with the board and to write some opinions from a center–left partisan view to demonstrate the newspaper's intent to have a broad perspective and to model journalistic dialogue civility with the editor. This participation resulted in a series of roughly monthly opinions on a wide range of major issues.

The overarching theological framework for this effort is Karl Barth's admonition that Christians should figuratively carry a Bible in one hand and a newspaper in the other, always seeking to interpret the news in the light of the Bible rather than vice versa. Barth believed that such a witness would better the world. Barth was a contemporary of German theologian Dietrich Bonhoeffer and he obviously had Bonhoeffer's martyrdom for opposing Hitler in mind. In his book, *Dogmatics in Outline,* Barth noted that in 1933 the Evangelical Church in Germany seemed healthy but it was ineffective because, in his view, there was not *translation* of its message and theology into "language of the newspaper."

Almost all of my published opinions were responses to opinions of others, thereby representing the national partisan divide. Every opinion had a biblical perspective in mind, although this relationship was explicit in only about thirty percent of those published. Seven of my opinions published in the Minneapolis *Star Tribune* are also included in the review. I began filing these opinions into separate subject categories, which over time ended up with over one hundred opinions filed in the following ten categories: biblical interpretation, health care, human sexuality, gun violence, global warming, refugees, politics, economics, foreign policy, and war with its related issues of torture and terrorism.

The first two chapters provide some biblical or theological background. Five theological themes are reviewed in order to provide some sense of where I am in the spectrum of biblical interpretation. The third chapter is a review of biblical engagement with each news category in the form of published opinion responses. Each category starts with a section on biblical texts of reference ("Bible in one hand") followed by a section review of opinions that interpret the news ("Newspaper in One Hand"). The fourth and fifth chapters consider some history of American Christianity since 1950 as background for looking at what changes might be realistically considered going forward.

My view is that change from traditional views of faith and politics is called for but will not be easy because in the last century, congregational Christianity in the United States has demonstrated considerable reluctance to engage in public political dialogue over differences as a witness of the Barth–Bonhoeffer type. There are many obstacles to such change and perhaps there never was much such emphasis, but American Christianity seems increasingly irrelevant to many Americans. Unusual times may call for change.

The purpose of this analysis–review is not to encourage Christians to do more newspaper editorial writing because of some presumed positive potential. There is little such potential simply because there is little available editorial space. Therefore other venue options should be considered. There are risks in congregational attempts to address the broad range of public issues with significant moral components. But there are also potential benefits. Studies have shown that in the US, younger generations are not joining Christian churches because Christianity seems irrelevant to many of the injustice and stewardship issues of the twenty-first century. For them, congregations could become more attractive if they functioned as centers for civil moral deliberation.

Reporting on this project is also not to suggest that it demonstrates some unique journalism or political stance or theology. Many others could do those things better. Any implied uniqueness is simply a documentation of what seems rare in American church and political life, that is, attempts at a Barth–Bonhoeffer type of Christian witness that engages a full range of controversial political issues with biblical texts in a public forum.

To whatever extent this review may stimulate some effort to make the Bible more effectively relevant to all of American life, my experience is provided as a hoped-for contribution to that end.

CHAPTER 1

Introduction

Barth and Bonhoeffer

MOST CHRISTIANS KNOW THAT Dietrich Bonhoeffer was a German theologian and pastor who publicly spoke out against Hitler as early as 1933, and they know that he was executed on Hitler's orders a short time before the prison he was held in was liberated in 1945. I had a life-long interest in biblical theology and first learned of Bonhoeffer in college. His writings have had a strong influence on my interest in, and practice of, faith.

A short time after discovering Bonhoeffer I also learned about his friend, prominent Swiss theologian, Karl Barth. I didn't read Barth as much as Bonhoeffer, but I came across his well- known advice to theological students: Christians should figuratively carry a Bible in one hand and newspaper in the other, but in relating the two, care should always be taken to interpret current events in the light of the Bible rather than the other way around.[1] Barth had high regard for newspapers in his time, and he had reporters and journalists relatively high on his prayer lists. This discipline obviously requires searching for texts relevant to newsworthy topics.

This seemed like good theological advice, and I wondered if in formulating it, Barth might have been thinking about what had happened in Germany under Adolph Hitler. I found a likely answer in what he said about the Lutheran church in Germany under Hitler in the fourth chapter of his book, *Dogmatics in Outline*:

---

1. Hall, *The Steward*, 22. Bibliography (See Also *Time Magazine, Bibliography*)

There must be *translation*, for example, into the language of the newspaper . . . Let us beware of remaining stuck where we are and refusing to advance into the world to meet worldly attitudes. For instance, in 1933 in Germany there was plenty of serious, profound, and living Christianity and confession—God be praised and thanked! But unfortunately, this confession remained imbedded in the language of the church and did not translate into the political attitude demanded at the time in which it would have become clear that the Evangelical Church had to say 'No' to National Socialism . . . It was not capable of that and the results are open to the day. Think what would have happened had the Evangelical Church at that time had expressed its church knowledge in the form of a worldly political attitude. A church not clear on having this duty would a priori betake itself to the graveyard . . . May every individual Christian be clear that so long as his faith is in a snail's shell . . . he has not yet come to believe. [2]

This Barth statement should be considered in the context of many statements by Bonhoeffer, such as the following question he posed in his unfinished book, *Ethics:* "Has the Church merely to gather up those whom the wheel has crushed or has she to prevent the wheel from crushing them?"[3]

Taken together, such statements by these two theologians can be reasonably interpreted to mean that Christians, either as individuals or collectively, should be in the business of dialogue in attempting to communicate the Bible's relationship to major political issues, especially those with obvious moral dimensions. Consistent with the US Constitution, this doesn't mean that pastors should endorse candidates, but the law shouldn't prohibit conversation about issues separate from candidates. This could especially apply to adult forums and Bible studies. The haunting question ever since the tragedy of the Holocaust remains: Could a similar massive implosion of morality occur anywhere, anytime?

The Bible is Political

To expect a widespread practice of Bible–newspaper dialogue in Christian congregations seems unrealistic, but I unexpectedly had a rare opportunity to attempt such a discipline on my own. A few years after my wife and I

2. Barth, *Dogmatics in Outline.* 33. *Bibliography*
3. Bonhoeffer, *Ethics,* 321. *Bibliography*

retired to our lake home near Brainerd, Minnesota, some letters began to appear in the Brainerd Dispatch that were critical of the discussions that the Evangelical Lutheran Church in America (ELCA) was having on homosexuality. These criticisms of the ELCA were clustered just before and after the 2009 Church-wide Assembly that approved welcoming gay and lesbian persons into the church. Some of these opinions seriously misrepresented the process, which prompted me to write some rebuttal letters that the Dispatch published.

Not long after, the Affordable Care Act (ACA) was introduced and became prominent in the news and was debated on the editorial pages of the Dispatch. As a physician, I had a natural professional interest in health care delivery reform. In addition, from 2009 through 2012 there were several mass shootings in the US. This kept gun violence and possible tighter gun control in the news. I had served two years in the U.S Army medical corps during the Viet Nam war, I had also served on a jury in a gun store robbery-murder case, and like most medical specialties, the American College of Physicians had published position papers on gun control. Therefore, I submitted some opinions on these issues. This began a series of roughly monthly publications that evolved into a wider range of newsworthy subjects.

In 2012, the editor of the Dispatch asked me to serve a term as a community representative on its editorial board. Part of my role was to write some left-of-center opinions to constructively counter this editor's conservative, partisan position. This was partly in order to demonstrate his commitment to have the newspaper represent both political sides while he could editorialize his. I saw this as a uniquely positive opportunity and accepted this position with the understanding that we would commit to write in a manner that would exemplify respectful dialogue. I continued to write about once a month after I left the position. Over an eight-year period, ninety-six of my letters and opinion-length submissions were published.

Some of my scientific perspectives on homosexuality and gun violence had been published in Minneapolis papers and theological journals back as far as the early 1990s. Partly to document that my interest in these issues did not start with my Dispatch experience, these opinions were added to my list. In all opinions, I had Barth's perspective on biblical relevance always in mind, although a biblical perspective was explicit in about one-third of the opinions.

In recent decades, I read some books by theologian Marcus Borg, who was a professor in the philosophy department at Oregon State University where he taught Christian theology. In that setting of highly skeptical students, he pushed the traditional theological envelope in a number of ways, including biblical interpretation of a historical–metaphorical approach rather than literal-factual. Borg also promoted a non-violent political–activist application of biblical theology to current temporal issues. His last book, *Convictions,* has an entire chapter titled, "The Bible is Political."[4] Thus Barth, Bonhoeffer, and Borg came together to frame my theological thinking on contemporary moral issues.

Cheap Grace and Two-sphere Ethics

What seems conspicuously obvious, but little spoken of, is how strikingly rare Barth's recommendation is openly followed in Christian congregations or promoted in seminaries. In an Internet web search, I found an ELCA Lutheran pastor's "Behind the scenes of the sermon" blog titled, "Why it's time to retire 'The Bible in one hand, the newspaper in the other.'" His reasons were summarized under paragraph titles such as "Who reads newspapers anymore?" and, "Should preachers really be putting this much trust in the mainstream media"? This pastor blamed the press for his decision to not engage contemporary major issues. Such arguments are weak enough to suggest there are also other factors behind his dismissal of Barth's advice.

A retired pastor that I know well told me that because he expressed his opposition to the Gulf war in a sermon, four prominent members of his congregation promptly left the congregation. Over the years, some other pastors, including college friends, made comments to me such as, "Last Sunday I felt like I preached like a false prophet." These pastors thought that they should have used one of the lectionary texts to address an important problem facing the nation or community. But they were inhibited for "political" reasons. A parishioner leaving church might remark, "I'd recommend you stick to the gospel, pastor." The pastoral concern was that donor support or membership might be adversely affected if controversial issues with political overtones turned up in sermons.

Assuming admonitions such as those of Barth, Bonhoeffer, and Borg have validity, a relevant question is whether or not this issue should be regarded as purely a clergy issue that leaves laypersons off the hook, given the

4. Borg, *Convictions,* 147–68. *Bibliography*

difficulties pastors may face. It can be argued that laity involvement should be expected, a decision I came to in college—strongly influenced by a layman in my home congregation followed by some college professors.

In the years that I was a student at St. Olaf College, one morning chapel service a week had a senior student give a ten-minute message. I recall one student who quoted a paragraph from Bonhoeffer's book, *The Cost of Discipleship*, first published in Germany in 1937 during Hitler's ascent to power. It impressed me in a way that I never forgot: "We Lutherans have gathered like eagles round the carcass of cheap grace, and there we have drunk the poison which has killed the life of following Christ."[5]

This statement led me to read more Bonhoeffer, including his *Ethics*. In that book, he criticized a defective sacred vs. secular system of "two sphere" ethics that was commonly practiced instead of the more biblical "one-sphere" holistic Christian ethic calling Christians to be good stewards of all life relationships with Christ at the center.[6] Bonhoeffer asserted that the Christian ethics of his day made churches places where drunkards and adulterers could be converted, but where church members didn't develop the courage to speak out about the evils of his generation.

The obvious limitation of newspapers in making a Christian witness of a Barth--Bonhoeffer type is the limited editorial space available for public dialogue, especially for non-professional writers. My opportunity was unique and rare. This limitation generates questions about what could and should be the role of congregations in sponsoring public dialogues on biblical relevance to major issues challenging the nation.

Religion Kills!

This analysis assumes strong theological validity for the Barth Bible–newspaper admonition cited here. One should pause, however, and acknowledge that many Christians may differ with this Barth-Bonhoeffer-Borg formulation, arguing that politically related topics distract from the core mission of the church to proclaim the gospel message. Such views appeared in local newspapers, including at least two by a syndicated columnist.

All of the foregoing questions should be considered in the broad American context of declining credibility of religion in general, and organized Christianity in particular. Surveys have shown that agnostics and

5. Bonhoeffer, *The Cost of Discipleship*, 47. *Bibliography*

6. Bonhoeffer, *Ethics*, 196–207. *Bibliography*

atheists have been increasing, although not as rapid as groups with persons that define their religious affiliation as "none" (no religious preference). It can be argued both that such trends are due to excessive engagement of socio-political issues or due to the lack of constructive engagement.

As of this writing, the "nones" are about 25% of American society, and most of them describe themselves as "spiritual but not religious."[7] These Americans claim to be ethically conscientious and active in environmental and justice issues, partly because they do not see organized religion as active enough to deserve their time and money. I can understand why nones might ask, "Why don't most of you Christians live as if you take the Bible seriously?" My experience could be considered an experiment in Barth's call to seriously move the Bible into the realities of the world to demonstrate to the "spiritual but not religious" that critical moral engagement of public issues is not considered biblically out of bounds by some very respected theologians. Furthermore, these trends suggest the need for a new theological turn in Christian mission and ministry. This book suggests a possible, if unlikely, new emphasis.

In my view, there have been serious theological challenges directed at major moral issues in the Barth mode, but most seeming to not get very far out of academia. For example, in the introduction of one of his books, published in early 2003, theologian Douglas John Hall made reference to two words scrawled in large letters on a graffiti–inviting outer wall of the Presbyterian College of Montreal. The words were, "Religion Kills."[8] After acknowledging that there is truth in this declaration, Hall went on to warn that the then-planned invasion of Iraq by the nation that claimed to be the most self–avowed Christian in the world would only make the hostility that produced the attack worse. The subsequent decade of history proved this prediction to be true. Hall is recognized primarily for his insightful publications of Luther's theology of the cross, so I do not regard him as some fringe theologian taking a partisan stance.

Few Christians, however, seem to have noted how accurate this warning from Hall was, although cynics would likely say his statement was just a lucky stab. But similar statements opposing the war were made by the World Council of Churches, the Pope at the time, and many other Christian world leaders. The reality is that at the time, about 60 percent of American

7. Putnam and Campbell, *American Grace,* 123. *Bibliography*

8. Hall, *The Cross in Our Context,* 1–5. *Bibliography*

Christians supported the invasion of Iraq, although support for the war faded quite quickly.

But what of the epithet, "religion kills!"? Hall quotes an American journalist who suggested that the question of a relationship of actions such as killing to any theologies is unanswerable or irrelevant— "religion is only "the essence of abstraction." The journalist claimed that religion is really only concerned about other-world matters. However, Americans seem to have little trouble linking killing with Islam but not with Christianity. Christians should have difficulty with this "only an abstraction" notion since Jesus is the one who said, "By their fruits you will know them." (Matthew 7:20) Hall's conclusion is that, "The foundational beliefs of a religious faith will find expression in one way or another, in the deeds and deportment of its membership." And the "religion kills" slogan are "words to which every religious person and institution in these times ought to pay close and thoughtful attention."[9]

Almost exactly thirteen years after the book by Hall was published, a guest opinion in the *New York Times* by evangelists Shane Claiborne and Tony Campolo was titled, "The Evangelicalism of Old White Men is Dead."[10] His opinion asserted that, President Trump's election "pulled the roof off" of the house they had called home. Such facts reflect the contrasting faces of American Christianity that cripple the credibility of its witness. In this context, should skeptical observers outside of the Church be blamed for wondering if Christians know what biblical morality stands for?

Wrong Belief

The Christian Ethics course that I had in college was taught by Harold Ditmanson, a highly-respected professor honored by naming an addition to the college library after him. My term paper for that course was titled "Professional Laypersons," which was a sort of oxymoron title that combined two words that alone designate separate or opposite categories of vocation. The core theme was that laity might not be professional in the same way as clergy are, but we should take our Christian responsibilities in church and society as seriously as clergy do.

The Scripture text I related to the theme was a conflation of two verses from Second Timothy: "Do your best to present yourself to God as one

9. Ibid., 1–4

10. Campolo and Claiborne, *New York Times* editorial, *Bibliography*

approved, a workman who has no need to be ashamed . . . for God did not give us a spirit of timidity, but a spirit of power and love and self–control." (2 Timothy 2:15, 1:7) For the rest of my life I attempted to daily remind myself of this "Do your best" theme. The broader question is whether or not we, as American Christians, have been doing our best in relating the Bible to the realities of serious issues that we have had to confront, some of which our country generated.

Bonhoeffer warned of a perverted Christianity that he called cheap grace—accepting a precious gift but treating it like trash. Karl Barth warned of a perversion with a different name. In the chapter cited earlier in his *Dogmatics in Outline* Barth described faith as a confession and a decision. To summarize,

> Faith is the decision in which men have the freedom to be publicly responsible, not only for their trust in God's Word and for their knowledge of the truth of Jesus Christ in the language of the Church, but also in worldly attitudes, and above all in their actions and conduct. As related to this Confession, the Church is a community distinguished from the world, in it and a part of it, yet not of it. But faith is not only a decision in choosing between belief and unbelief. It is seeking to make sure faith is authentic as distinct from unintended wrong belief or superstition.[11]

Barth also states that authentic faith is not limited to the language of faith heard in the "area of the church." It is also related to actions in the world: "in the village or in a city, beside the school, the cinema and the railway station." The message in these words for our time should be that Christians, both as individuals and in organized church groups, must be in constant "self-examination" (to borrow words from Kierkegaard). This discipline should be to maintain certainty that we not become self-deceived by thinking authentic faith only requires living under a label of being members of a Christian community in a Christian nation. This could be one example of wrong belief.

A dictionary definition of superstition is "irrational belief in a thing or circumstance." Based on this, some skeptics would claim any religion is irrational. But both Martin Luther and the Catholic Church have distinguished superstition in general from superstition among Christians.

A basic biblical reference related to a superstition defect is Matthew 23:16–24. Jesus refers here to practices in which certain rules are selected

---

11. Barth, *Dogmatics in Outline*, 28–30. *Bibliography*

by religious people as a means of circumventing "weightier matters of the law," such as "justice, mercy, and faith." This fits with the concept that faith should be a holistic matter involving all of life–relationships, not making a priority of a few to the exclusion of others. In other words, certain selective practices of faith can become superstitions, which are biblically judged as defective, both regarding faith and lack of positive effects on the world and its governance. A major question implicit in this review is whether or not Christians on different sides of an issue can live together with the differences while continuing indefinite constructive dialogue.

"What If?"

In the first section of this chapter, part of what I quoted from Karl Barth's *Dogmatics in Outline was*, "Think what would have happened had the Evangelical Church at that time . . . ?" Barth could have asked the question starting with the words, "*What if . . . ?*"

In the process of my opinion writing, other "what if?" questions emerged: What if most Christians in America could dialogue person–to–person the way readers can do in print on newspaper editorial pages? What if a wide range of prophetic biblical themes on societal issues articulated by respected theologians were given significant emphasis in well–attended forums in most churches? What if these sessions produced position papers of agreement or alternatives that could be presented to elected officials for pending or possible legislation? In short, what if we took what the Bible says seriously according to some of the world's most respected theologians? Might not the moral fabric of our country and politics be better?

The theologians I was most familiar with included Barth, Bonhoeffer, Borg, Bright, Bruggemann, Hall, Niebuhr, and Tillich. I incorporated some of their views in my writing. This book gives a snapshot glimpse of this experience, for as much or little potential it may have for American Christianity.

Word limitations make newspaper efforts vulnerable to criticism of "sound-bite theology," and newspapers admittedly have word limitations. One possible solution could be to create venues with few dialogue space limits. Para-church organizations with arms–length denominational distance from congregations similar to the Knights of Columbus relationship to the Catholic Church, and Wheat Ridge Ministries (formerly Wheat Ridge Foundation) to the Lutheran Church Missouri Synod could be organized for dialogue purposes. I was part of a group, "Lutheran Episcopal Dialogue of Minnesota," which was an advocacy group for full communion with the Episcopal Church (ratified in 1999).

Critics might also allege that it is not proper for amateur theologians to be grappling with writings of professional theologians. I could agree. But the solution for that liability would be for more professionals to be involved. Someone could explore what Karl Barth may have meant by "There must be *translation*, for example, into the language of the newspaper." It would also be helpful if laypersons would speak out against threatened member–resignation or reduced financial support of religious institutions if they get too close to partisan issues. Such actions stifle willingness to dialogue.

I regard my political stance as center-left, not because it started from some such ideology and remained there. I consider most major issues to have moral components if looked for, and on most of these the moral dimension can be related to the Bible. A position formulated in this context can then be secondarily defined politically by how it matches current partisan criteria. Over my lifetime this process has moved me politically from right of center to left of center. I hold these positions not primarily to prove their superiority, but to serve as some starting points in discussion or challenges for debate.

In summary and as stated in the Preface, the purpose of this book is not to suggest some unique theology, or journalism, political stance, or individual effort. The main purpose is simply documentation of attempts at what seems relatively rare in American church and political life: to engage major controversial societal issues in a biblical context in a public forum.

The foundational biblical basis for this engagement is that outcomes of issues should be in line with what many of the major prophetic voices in the biblical record did: Moses' speaking to a Pharaoh, Nathan to David, the prophets to their people, Jesus to Pilate, and Paul to Festus and Agrippa. These were all representatives of one kingdom speaking to another. Right belief is not just a call to claim belief in God. It is to also represent that God as a moral being concerned with moral issues in the world.

Organization and Road Map

An early question in considering a report on my newspaper opinion experience was how to best analyze and present scores of opinions on a wide range of subjects. The first step of separating the opinions into different categories was simple because for years I had been filing all of my opinions into what evolved to ten categories. These ten subject categories are biblical interpretation, health care, sexuality, global warming, gun violence, war (including torture and terrorism), refugees, politics, economics, and foreign policy. Republishing all original opinions was briefly considered. However, the large number of pages required for this would shift emphasis to journalism nuances, detracting from the book's main purpose. That theme is to encourage Christians to more constructive dialogue on partisan and theological differences in venues other than newspapers.

A brief overview of all opinion titles divided into the ten subject categories is displayed in Appendix A. The subject categories are designated by alphabetic letters and the opinions titles in each category have a number designation. For example, the opinion "Obamacare is a First Step" is referenced in chapter 3 with a (B-11) endnote. Appendix B has selected original opinions with the same letter–number designations. The appendices are reader options not regarded as essential to the book's main theme. Subject designation of many opinions is somewhat arbitrary because many opinions could be placed in more than one category.

In summary, the three major themes of this book are:

1. American Christians have largely rejected or failed substantive engagement of major newsworthy moral issues when there are credible arguments for doing so.

2. My attempt to follow Barth's admonition using newspaper editorial space has little potential for expanded effectiveness because of space limitations.

3. This report is less to argue the superiority of a partisan stance or utilize newspapers than it is to challenge Christians to engage in similar civil debate in a different venue.

Stated another way, what churches are doing in moral deliberation would be much better as positive major news that provoked professional editorials rather than attempting to have Christians get more opinions published on editorial pages. The Florida student's newsworthy protests against gun violence are good examples.

A roadmap through this analysis begins with a review of five theological themes that I attempt to keep in mind when—as if descending into a valley—I attempt to make biblically related moral judgments about "worldly" news events. The focus then moves into a valley of concrete issues where

Bible engages news in a review of selected opinions in all ten subject categories (Chapter 3). Following this, attention moves back up the hill through a brief historical review of recent US Christianity. The journey ends in a return to theological emphases on repentance, and the importance of living a God–fearing life (Chapter 5).

Trumpism could have been a designated chapter. However, it was given separate status as a postscript to signify President Trump's entrance into a scheme not designed because of him, but unintentionally readymade to facilitate making some judgments about him. Mixing his statements and conduct with the usual less stark and more civil give and take discussion seemed distractive. It also seemed inappropriate to regard Trump as representative of most conservative or Republican philosophy.

Less than one-third of the opinions had an explicit biblical or theological connection because I do not think it appropriate to squeeze God or Jesus into every conversation. My frame of thinking in daily life is that one should first of all, "Be ready to give an answer to the hope that is within us," rather than explicitly impact every conversation. (1 Peter 3:15)

Most of the opinions in this report were responses to opinions someone else had written, including editors, syndicated journalists and readers. The complete list of opinions was computer–filed; most opinions were also saved in newsprint form. The word "Dispatch" always designates *Brainerd Dispatch*. About thirty percent of the opinions are about 750 words in length and the others are letter–length 300 words or less. The Dispatch allowed the longer opinion length submissions by readers until 2016, when this policy was discontinued, except for authors who had special expertise on a subject. Except for candidates or elected officials, any local names in republished original opinions were replaced with pronouns. A few opinion titles were altered to better indicate their subject content in the table of titles.

CHAPTER 2

Interpreting the Bible

Five Theological Themes

THE BIBLE HAS A special relationship to my opinion writing, not just because Karl Barth suggested it, but because it is the basis of Christian ethics in terms of law, prophets, and Jesus' teaching. This understanding should be expected of Christians. A problem comes, however, with interpretation. The Bible has acquired a reputation that it can be interpreted to justify almost anything. In order to provide some understanding of my interpretation priority guidelines for this project, this chapter outlines five special themes.

These themes are:

1. Martin Luther's theology of the cross as distinguished from its frequent corruptions.

2. Some of the explicit societal indictments of the Old Testament prophets.

3. The biblical concept of living as God's stewards of all life-relationships.

4. Living in two realms or kingdoms.

5. The anti-biblical themes in Ayn Rand's popular political-economic philosophy.

The first four of the above theological themes are directly related to the Bible. These may be regarded metaphorically as four walls of a hearing room, each representing a different biblical perspective from which to begin examination of the moral aspects of some newsworthy issue or person. In contrast, the fifth theme of Ayn Rand's philosophy is an example of a political ideology that I, like many if not most Christians who are familiar with Rand, regard as anti-biblical. Ayn Rand's philosophy will be briefly reviewed, which will make its anti-religious, agnostic, and amoral themes obvious. Her philosophy is theological in that it refers to God and religions, although it does so in a negative or atheist perspective. In spite of this anti–Christian quality, Rand's philosophy has been promoted and practiced by many prominent U.S. politicians, including some who claim to be Christian. Many who may not even know Rand espouse ideologies that closely match hers.

In the application of these themes, one may have more relevance to what is under scrutiny than others, or all may have some relevance to some entity. This design helps in further selection of biblical texts with more specific relevance to the subject of interest. The two–realm concept is not as objective or specifically helpful in judging current news issues as the other themes are, but I find it a good reminder of the difference between what is finite and temporal, and what the Bible claims is infinite and eternal.

My selected themes should not imply that they are better than any others that could be selected. My formulations should be expected to be most understandable to Christians who claim the Bible as their main authority for faith and life matters, and any judgments by Christians that differ from mine should ideally attempt a biblical basis for disagreement. Giving priority to the Bible as I do also does not preclude the reality that many persons who are skeptics, agnostics or atheists live more morally constrained lives than some avowed Christians.

Luther's Theology of the Cross

The "Great Reversal"

That Jesus was crucified by Roman soldiers is such an undoubted fact that anyone who chooses to examine the significance of Jesus in history and for our time must deal with it. Wherever we find the cross, whether on flags, buildings, jewelry, or bumper stickers, everyone knows that it refers to the cross on which Jesus died. Numberless and nameless are the Jews crucified by Roman soldiers, but for two millennia, the cross has meant the cross on which Jesus died. Jesus was a carpenter's son from Nazareth, a town so obscure that for centuries only the gospels mentioned it.

The cross has had continued historic influence, not because people remember how Jesus was put to death, but because how Jesus was put to death has been especially influential. The cross may have many meanings, but one of its foremost is the theological meaning of the Christian understanding of God. One of the primary, if not the primary, unexpected, and paradoxical meaning that the cross reveals about the Creator of the universe, is that this God is a God who suffers. God suffers with and for God's creation. If there are degrees in God's suffering, God may suffer most for those persons who innocently suffer the most, especially when at the hands of others. This, in turn, is what should be a primary focus of those who claim to believe in this God and claim to be followers of Jesus.

According to the New Testament message, a positive human relationship with God might not theologically require works for justification, but good works are natural "fruits"—evidence of an authentic response of faith. (Matthew 7:20) The related question here regards how different understandings of the cross may differently affect life in the temporal world. Religion can blind rather than open eyes to the needs of others.

In the gospels, Peter James and John did not want to come down from the Mount of Transfiguration. When Jesus said that he must go to Jerusalem to suffer and die, Peter objected, drawing a rebuke from Jesus. Peter seemed to want to be a part of a new power coalition against other powers of the world. But the cross event resulted in what Professor Douglas John Hall calls "the great reversal" of previous theological conceptions of God. Ever since the early Church, cross theology has had to contend with alternate theological formulations that prefer to look away from the suffering cross reality while retaining it as a symbol. With this comes a turning away from persons suffering in this world.

A major factor that encourages biblical theologies that turn away from the cross is the human participation in worldly affluence and power. One of the first major examples in post-biblical times occurred in 330 CE when Constantine made Christianity the official religion of the Roman Empire. Constantine allegedly even saw a sign of the cross in the sky, along with words, "In this sign conquer." Thus began the era of cultural Christianity collaborating with power known as "Christendom," when the church became culturally "established" in contrast to the servant ministry of an oppressed minority religion that it was primarily known by in the first three centuries. Constantine's move was "up to" what Luther called a corrupted theology of worldly power and glory. In his time this was most evident in a church linked with state raising money for a cathedral by selling indulgences. This corruption has also been called triumphalism.

In the book of Acts, the unique cultural feature of the first gatherings together of Christians was socio-economic equality. In the ancient letter to Diogenetus written by someone sent out from Rome to investigate what kind of people Christians were, a key representative sentence was, "They share their food but not their wives." Participation in government is not bad, but the Christian push should be against the temptation to use politics to gain power for individuals or certain groups in promoting Christianity at the expense of caring for those in need. Abraham Lincoln once said, "Nearly all men can stand adversity. If you want to test a man's character, give him power."

There is glory and triumph in the gospel proclamation, but this glory is paradoxical and often more hidden rather than obvious. It is not what the world thinks of as glory. Just as it is illogical to expect that an omnipotent power would demonstrate this power through an ignoble death of an innocent person as a criminal, it is illogical to think that one of the keys to the health and longevity of human individuals and societies might be related to how its people treat their most vulnerable members and neighbors. Who could have guessed that the same Peter who objected to Jesus' pronouncement that he would suffer, later was beaten for his witness and rejoiced with the other apostles that they "were worthy to suffer for the name." [Acts 5:41]

The story is told of a woman who had many children and was asked which one she loved or cared for the most. She answered that her love was focused on the child hurting the most at any given time. Jesus wants his followers to always be aware of those who suffer, in part to protect us against our own selfishness that can hinder our relationships with God and each other. Any religion that tries to insulate its adherents from suffering will enjoy temporary success, but as Dostoevsky insisted, "it will turn to ashes at the death of a child."

The "Great Refusal"

Although I had some understanding of Luther's theology of the cross over the years, the theologian whose writings most gripped me more recently was Professor Douglas John Hall, especially his book, *The Cross in Our Context*. Derived from the first twenty-one of Luther's ninety-five theses, Hall's summary is:

> The cross of Christ hides—and reveals—the decision of God to absorb in his own person the compulsions of the alienated human spirit to kill, and so to create "a new spirit within us," a spirit that has passed through death to the life that is possible on death's far side. [1]

This life with a new spirit received by grace through faith leads to rejection of the whole imperialistic bent of "established" Christendom linked with power and glory. There is no place in the world on the brink of self-destruction for a religion that is driven by the quest for power and glory. Such a religion can only be a part of the problem, not its solution. Glory theologies often are a synergistic melding of secular and political ideologies of power and coercion with Christian doctrine. A theology of the cross stance that identifies and opposes such theologies of glory has been dubbed "The Great Refusal" by authentic theologians of the cross.

Professor Hall contrasts authentic cross theology with the contending theology of glory with the three positive virtues named by Paul in 1 Corinthians 13, which he contends should be thought of and stated together with what they negate: "faith (not sight), hope (not consummation), love (not power)."[2] This is because part of our nature, pulled by the lure of our culture wants instead the "virtues" of sight, consummation, and power. Our human nature wants the false security promised by the false virtues, which ultimately undermines rather than strengthens the health and well-being of both individuals and the societies they are a part of. A core mission of Christianity should be to promote the counter-cultural message of the cross for the sake of the health and well-being of all in the here and now—not only for the sake of individual eternal destinies.

Another way Professor Hall distinguishes between an authentic theology of the cross and glory triumphalism is:

> Prophetic religion—or faith—as we have it exemplified in the tradition of Jerusalem (Amos, Isaiah, Jeremiah, etc.), engages in an ongoing critique of the purely human tendency to deify fondly held views of the individual or the group in religions (including Christianity as a religion). Such religion suffers badly from the

1. Hall, *The Cross in our Context*, 6. *Bibliography*
2. Ibid., 33

deep psychic need of finite humankind to find security and permanency in expressions of belief from which ambiguity, relativity, and doubt are expunged.[3]

Such expunging to re-mold faith results in unbiblical theologies of glory—theologies that attempt to "triumph" in this world through coercive means, whether by religious doctrines of intolerance or patriotic-nationalistic collaboration.

Luther was skeptical of "answering" theologies that gave in to the hubris of assuming closure by explaining the world too handily. They often end up with the transmutation of faith as trust (*fiducia*) into belief as assent to doctrinal propositions (*assensus*). Paradoxical systems such as those in the Bible do not assume such closure. It is paradoxical that one would assert, as Luther did, that at best humans are simultaneously justified and sinners. One often must keep one law at the expense of breaking another.

The means of proclaiming the cross should be nonviolent persuasion, not coercion. The Christian should be a political activist as Jesus was in critiquing society and speaking truth to power, but as much as possible without resorting to actual or threatened coercion. Governing systems must have police systems to enforce laws and defend against foreign enemies, but biblical pressure should always be in the non-violent direction. Two lines from the hymn "Lead On, O King Eternal" are relevant: "But not with swords loud clashing or stir of rolling drums; with deeds of love and mercy, the heavenly kingdom comes."

The prophetic nature of theology of the cross

One of the things that makes professor Hall's identification with the "prophetic religion" of an authentic theology of the cross is his own political prediction come true drawn from this theology. It is helpful to quote his words directly. In 2003, just before the US invasion of Iraq, Professor Hall made reference to a "Religion kills" epithet scrawled on an outer wall of the Presbyterian College of Montreal just after the events of 9/11. He then wrote:

> Christians—and especially Western Christians—who imagine that the epithet "Religion Kills" has no relevance to themselves or their religion are greatly deceived. Not only does the whole history

3. Ibid., 18.

of the Christian religion bear ample evidence of the accuracy of such a charge, and not only does the present-day world situation confirm the suspicion that Christianity has by no means repented of its propensity to aggressive behavior; but at a subtle yet more deadly level, the association of the Christian religion with white, Western/Northern economic, military, and cultural imperialism constitutes possibly the single most insidious cause of global peril. It can in fact be argued (and is) that the current bellicosity of the militant forms of Islam represents a reaction of the Muslim world to its humiliation by the powerful technocratic West, especially as the latter is embodied in the one remaining planetary super-power—which happens to be the most avowedly Christian of all the nations of the world. . .[4]

Professor Hall then points out that:

So long as the Christian faith is unable to distinguish itself at the level of foundational belief from the Western imperial peoples of which it has been and is inextricably linked, its actions and ethical claims will be ambiguous, even when they are inspired by Christian motives. As it is, thankfully, a significant (if not yet significant enough!) portion of Christian people on North America, Europe, and other traditionally Christian lands have participated in acts of disengagement from the present policies of their host societies—for example in the current protests of mainstream Christians in the United states and elsewhere of the evident desire of the governing authorities of America and its allies to undertake, with or without United Nations approval, a 'preventive' war against Iraq. All who discern the signs of the times and realize, therefore, that violence, even when it is called anti-terrorism, can beget only more violence—including more terrorism, must laud such acts of dissent from the dominant culture. But while such actions on the part of Christian persons and denominations are admirable, they are neither self-sustaining nor sufficiently far-reaching.[5]

Professor Hall's judgment, drawn deep from one of Luther's understandings of the crucifixion of Jesus, and the engagement of this theology with American worldly power, should be worth noting because of the accuracy of Hall's prediction about the Iraq war. This is especially noteworthy in his prediction that violence, even when it is called anti-terrorism, can beget only more violence, - including terrorism. The multiple attestations

4. Ibid., 3.
5. Ibid., 4–5.

invoking God as on our side seemed to border on tempting God, making it predictable that by biblical standards the war would not be as "quick, clean, and decisive" as its promoters promised.

Professor Hall is little in the news because of the truth in his prediction, but this should not be surprising. The Old Testament prophets were not popular in their day. They were fully honored only after it became known that their predictions came true. Hall shouldn't be singled out as uniquely alone because many other Christian leaders spoke out against that preemptive invasion. The same relevance can be applied to many other current issues. One factor that dulls perception of accurate predictions based on biblical sources is US patriotic nationalism linked mostly to the "evangelical" religious right. This faction can rightly be suspect of exemplifying Luther's definition of operating under a theology of glory rather than an authentic theology of the cross.

Theologians of the cross

Another dimension of the prophetic nature of the theology of the cross is in the distinction between a theology *about* the cross, and a theology *of* the cross. This, in turn relates to the distinction between being a *theologian* of the *cross* and a *theologian* of *glory*. The late Professor Gerhard Forde of Luther Seminary placed great emphasis on these distinctions. A *theology* is something that helps understand the nature of God. A *theologian* acts on it. Thesis 21 (of Luther's 95) is: "The theologian of glory calls evil good and good evil. The theologian of the cross calls a thing what it is." Part of Forde's explanation is: "We are not speaking here of being a 'professional' theologian. Indeed, being a theologian of the cross has nothing to do with might be called "academic" theology. . . theologians of the cross learn to call a spade a spade . . . Becoming a theologian of the cross involves turning to face the problems, joys, and sorrows of everyday life . . . Suffice it to say for now that all of us are theologians in one way or another." [6]

A paradox in the cross/glory formulation regards good works, or the law. Most Christians know that one cannot be justified by works, but good works, or "works of love" are expected as a witness to faith and evidence of gratitude for the gift of grace. But there is more to it than that. The first ten of Luther's 95 theses were on the problem of works. In almost shocking fashion, Thesis 3 states: "Although the works of man always seem attractive

6. Forde, *On Being a Theologian of the Cross*, 10, 71. *Bibliography*

and good, they are nevertheless likely to be mortal sins." In Forde's explanation, "A human work, no matter how good, is deadly sin because it in actual fact entices us away from naked trust in the grace of God to a trust in self."

My understanding is that this means we feel good about ourselves because of our works despite believing that we are saved by grace alone. We tend to slip into a "helping God" mode of thinking by adding coercive means to some perceived worthy goals, and before long are on a "glory road." We lose a sense of a reverent "awe" type of fear in God and God's grace. We cease to "call a thing what it is," especially when it is an individual or corporate sin. We start permitting sin, blinded by our often "selected" good works that make us feel worthy. We may think because we have "In God we Trust" printed on our money, and "one nation under God" in our Pledge of Allegiance, we are a "Christian nation." Might this be an example of the "wrong belief" Karl Barth referred to? (see introduction).

One difference I see between Forde's writing and Hall's is that Forde seems to consider only works of individual Christians in relationship to their faith. Hall may have viewed Luther's context of indulgences as an alleged "good works" involving the power (and glory) of the Holy Roman Empire linking Church and State. In a manner similar to Forde's individual faith, Hall focuses on the Western established Christendom with all of its power, which amounts to "triumphalism" or theologies of glory antithetical to a theology and true theologians of the cross. Americans may not have chosen this but are by citizenship participatory in it. In a chapter section on "The Crisis in Planetary Justice" in *The Cross in Our Context,* Hall quotes Dorothee Soelle: "There is life that is productive and worth living, and there is life that is economically useless. Twenty percent have the right to use, to exploit, and to throw away, while eighty percent are superfluous, the losers . . . " The US is part of the twenty percent living under a corporate and nationalist Christian theology of glory.

This American "technological Christendom" is not something entirely new in the last century. Professor Hall notes that in 1534, the French explorer Cartier sailed up the St. Lawrence river to a Native American village at the present site of Montreal and caused a rude cross to be driven into the ground at a high point in the terrain and by this gesture declared, "All this land now belongs to the king of France." This expression of a pure theology of glory was only seventeen years after Luther posted his theses on the triumphalist glory perversion of an authentically biblical theology of the cross.

Not sounding very optimistic, Hall noted that conventional Christianity may need to experience greater failure than has yet befallen it before it is ready to discard the accumulated assumptions, beliefs, and practices of sixteen centuries of establishment, and seriously explore such a radical alternative as is signaled by the theology of the cross tradition. This is Hall's way of "calling a thing what it is," even though it is not a very happy thought.

This prophetic tradition of speaking truth to power in the public square goes back much farther. It started about David's time in the Old Testament. To those prophets, we will now turn.

The Old Testament Prophets

Jesus identified primarily with the Old Testament prophets rather than other religious groups of his time, especially as noted in his first proclamations that started his public ministry as recorded in Luke's gospel. Most of us grew up thinking of the prophets only as the source of Old Testament predictions of Jesus as a coming Messiah. Much of this came from Handel's oratorio of that name. But a large part of the prophets' words in the Bible are indictments of the divided nations of Israel and Judah, and the prophets' predicted judgments against those nations in history. Prominent theologians consider this prophetic history to not only have been a relevant warning for their era, but also for all societies and nations of all times and places. Therefore, some of the most relevant texts are worth citing after briefly sketching their historical context.

When considering the relevance of the prophets to political issues, it is important to note that some of the Old Testament prophets' writings are related to the dynamics of the four most powerful other nations of that part of the world in their time. In the order of their major engagements with Abraham's descendants, these nations are Egypt, Assyria, Babylon (Chaldea), and Persia.

Egypt, of course, was the nation from which Moses led the descendants of Abraham out to Canaan in about 1300 BCE. Egypt was still on the scene in a smaller way 500 years later at the time of the prophets. After about 200 years of living as a "tribal confederacy" among a number of other tribes in Palestine, this form of government was replaced with a monarchy starting with Saul. David followed, and his leadership created a prosperous and relatively powerful state centered in Jerusalem.

However, the affluence of this success fueled increasing divisions and immorality of multiple types. When David's son and successor Solomon died around 920 BCE, the kingdom split in two: the northern kingdom of Israel and the southern kingdom of Judah. The northern kingdom lasted until about 720 BCE when it was conquered and destroyed by Assyria, never again to exist as a political entity. The Babylonian empire then subdued the Assyrians after which they destroyed Jerusalem and in 586 BCE took most of Judah's survivors into exile in Babylon. The exile lasted about fifty years, ending in 539 BCE when Cyrus of Persia conquered the Babylonians and released most exiles to return to Jerusalem and Palestine.

The classical prophets belong to the time of the divided kingdoms, the exile, and the return. The earliest of these prophets was Amos, who began speaking about 750 BCE. The latest spoke in about 100 years after the exile. The exile may be viewed as one of the four major milestones in Old Testament history, the other three being the call of Abraham, the Exodus, and the Davidic Kingdom. The classical prophets built on the earlier biblical understanding of God as a monotheistic moral being who controls nature and history. The prophets asserted that God was up to "a new thing," in what was going on, which was yet to be more completely revealed.

The radical nature of the prophets' message was that God had decided both earthly kingdoms had to be destroyed as judgment for their failure to honor divine expectations in a covenantal relationship. This was not because they failed to achieve perfection but because they didn't even seem to care (not even "grieving the ruin of Joseph"–Amos 6:6). The astounding assertion was that destruction would come at the hands of other nations that God temporarily retained to serve his ends, even though these nations did not recognize Israel's God. The metaphor of "light" as a description of prosperity became replaced with a period of "darkness" signifying apostasy. This darkness was similar to the prior history of slavery in Egypt, but darkness made it easier for people to better see the "light" of God's continuing faithfulness. A "refined" faithful "remnant" was preserved for a future witness and prophecy fulfillment. (Isaiah 10:21)

But God was also seemingly changing from a "warrior" God to a nonviolent "suffering servant" Messiah. (Isaiah 53) People of faith and obedience would be eligible for citizenship in an eternal kingdom "not of this world," even though blessings vs. judgments would continue in earthly kingdoms related to the same divine standards given in the law and proclaimed by the prophets.

The words of the prophets may be divided into seven categories:

1. The call from God to proclaim his message.
2. General indictments of the failings of Israel or Judah.
3. Specific failure indictments.
4. Predictions of coming geopolitical negative judgments.
5. Predictions of Judah's release by Persia from Babylonian captivity.
6. Prediction of a coming Messiah with intimations of eternal reality.
7. Statements about the nature of God.

The failure to keep the Covenant was in part placing selfish desire ahead of worshiping God not only in ceremony but also in moral lives. Only some of the explicit indictments of number 3, above, are listed here by category.

Excessive trust in weapons of power.

Woe to those who go down to Egypt for help and rely on horses,
Who trust in chariots because they are many
And horsemen because they are very strong,
But do not look to the Holy One of Israel or consult the Lord!
Isaiah 31:1

Because you have trusted in your chariots,
And in the multitude of your warriors,
Therefore the tumult of war shall arise among your people.
Hosea 10:13–1

Misuse of personal power.

Why have we fasted and you see it not?
Behold, you fast only to quarrel and to fight
And to hit with a wicked fist.
Isaiah 58:3–4.

Money power linked to financial dishonesty.

Hear this, you who trample upon the needy,
And bring the poor of the land to an end,
Saying, "When will the new moon be over?
that we may sell grain?
And the Sabbath . . .
that we may offer wheat for sale,
that we may make the epha small and
The shekel great,
And deal deceitfully with false balances?"
Amos 8: 4–5

Covetous acquisition of material things

Hear this word, you cows of Bashan, who are in the mountain of Samaria,
who oppress the poor, who crush the needy.
who say to your husbands, "Bring us some drinks!"
The Lord God has sworn by his holiness
that, behold the days are coming upon you,
when they will take you away with hooks,
even the last of you with fishhooks."
Amos 4:1 5

Woe to you, who are complacent in Zion,
and to you who feel secure on Mount Samaria . . .
Woe to you who lie of beds of ivory,
and stretch themselves upon their couches,
and eat lambs from the flock,
and calves from the midst of their stall;
and sing idle songs from the sound of the harp,
and like David invent for themselves instruments of music;
who drink wine in bowels,
and anoint themselves with finest oils,
but are not grieved with the death of Joseph!
Therefore they shall be among the first of those to go into exile.

Your feasting and lounging will end.
Amos 6:1, 4–7

Woe to you who join house to house and add field to field,
Until there is no more room, and you are left to dwell alone
In the midst of the land.
Surely the great houses will become desolate
And fine mansions left without occupants.
Isaiah 5: 8–10

Ephraim has said, "Ah, but I am rich, I have gained wealth for myself";
but all the riches cannot offset the guilt he has incurred.
Hosea, 12:7–9

Like a basket full of birds, their houses are full of treachery;
They have grown fat and sleek.
Jeremiah 5:27

Dishonesty in the market place.

Woe to those who decree iniquitous decrees,
and the writers who keep writing oppression,
to turn aside the needy from justice and to rob the poor people of
their right,
that widows may be their spoil,
and that they may make the fatherless their prey!
Isaiah 10: 1–3; 5–6

Justice is turned back,
and righteousness stands afar off.
for truth has fallen in the public squares,
and righteousness cannot enter.
Isaiah 59:14

An appalling and horrible thing
has happened in the land.
The prophets prophesy falsely,
and the priests rule at their direction;

my people love to have it so,

 but what will you do when the end comes?

Jeremiah 5:30–31

Behold, you trust in deceptive words to no avail. Will you steal, murder, commit adultery, swear falsely, burn incense to Baal . . . and come and stand before me in this house, which is called by my name and say, 'We are delivered!'—only to go on doing these abominations? Has this house, which is called by my name, become a den of robbers in your eyes?

Jeremiah 7:5–11

Is there no balm in Gilead? Is there no physician there?

They bend their tongue like a bow . . .

falsehood and not truth has grown strong in the land;

for they proceed from evil to evil, and they do not know me, says the Lord

Jeremiah 8:22; 9:3

A trader, in whose hands are false balances, he loves to oppress.

Hosea 12:2

Disregard for the powerless poor.

They hate him who reproves in the gate,

and abhor him who speaks the truth.

Therefore because you trample upon the poor

And take from him exactions of wheat,

you have built houses of stone,

but you shall not dwell in them.

Amos 5:10–12

Hear this, you who trample upon the needy,

and bring the poor of the land to an end,

saying, "When will the moon be over . . . that we may buy the poor for silver

and the needy for a pair of sandals

and sell the refuse of the wheat."

Amos 8:4–6

Woe to those who decree iniquitous decrees,
And the writers who keep writing oppression,
to turn aside the needy from justice
And to rob the poor of my people of their right,
That widows may be their spoil.
And that they may make the fatherless their prey!
Ah, Assyria, the rod of my anger,
The staff of my fury
Against a godless nation I send him.
Isaiah 10:1–2; 5–6

Also on your skirts are found the lifeblood of guiltless poor;
You did not find them breaking in.
Yet in spite of these things
You say, 'I am innocent;
surely his anger has turned from me.
Behold, I will bring you to judgment
For saying, 'I have not sinned.
Jeremiah 2: 34,35

They judge not with justice with the fatherless to prosper,
And they do not defend the rights of the needy
Jeremiah 5:28

Disregard for widows, orphans, aliens, and sojourners (refugees).

For if you truly amend your ways and your doings, if you truly execute justice one with another, if you do not oppress the alien, the fatherless, and the widow, or shed innocent blood . . . then I will let you dwell in this place.
Jeremiah 7:6–7

Thus says the Lord: Do justice and righteousness, and deliver from the hand of the oppressor him who has been robbed. And do no wrong or violence to the alien, the fatherless, nor the widow, nor shed innocent blood in this place.
Jeremiah 22:3

Behold, the princes of Israel in you, every one according to his power, have been bent on shedding blood. Father and mother are treated with contempt in you; the sojourner suffers extortion in your midst; the fatherless and the widow are wronged in you.
Ezekiel 22: 6–7

Then I will draw near to you for judgment; I will be a swift witness against the sorcerers, against the adulterers, against those who swear falsely against those who oppress the hireling in his wages, the widow and the orphan, against those who thrust aside the sojourner, and do not fear me, says the Lord of hosts.
Malachi 3:5

Sexual immorality

When I fed them to the full, they committed adultery,
and trooped to the houses of harlots.
They were well-fed stallions, each neighing for his neighbor's wife.
Jeremiah 5: 7–8

One commits abomination with his neighbor's wife,
another defiles his daughter- in–law
Ezekiel 22:11

Contemporary Relevance of Prophets

The above indictments were against the Kingdoms of Israel and Judah between 800 and 500 BCE. It seems fair to say the indictments were as much against the populace as against their leaders. An obvious question is whether or not these messages for moral life in this temporal world are relevant to the United States in the twenty-first century. Multiple prominent theologians say "yes."

John Bright, in *The Kingdom of God* states, "We might ask to what extent Amos' indictment of society is applicable to us today. . . It is fully applicable. It takes no skill to point out that our society, like that of ancient Israel, is shot through with that which Amos denounced; injustice and greed, pleasure-loving ease, and venality. The indictment of Amos is an indictment of all societies, including our own" [7]

Similarly, in *Journey to the Common Good*, Walter Bruggemann writes: "The lines from Jeremiah well characterize the aggressive acquisitiveness that has marked the U.S. economy for a generation with a shameless greed at the expense of the neighbor . . . While the prophet saw all this a long time ago, it is now abundantly clear that our society has, until now learned very little, even though the covenantal, prophetic alternative of love, justice, and righteousness remains an offer. The most elemental passion of the prophetic tradition assumes that evangelical faith has little to do with private piety and everything to do with the systemic maintenance of a humane infrastructure." [8]

James Limburg, emeritus professor of Old Testament at Luther Seminary, in *The Prophets and the Powerless*, has this to say about the contemporary relevance of the prophets: "We must listen to them first of all in their own historical and geographic setting. But when we listen, we discover that their words refuse to be confined to these times and places . . . These prophets call a People of God who have been radically loved to become radical lovers of the powerless. They warn us against the arrogance that tends to accompany national or individual power and warn us to the indifference that accompanies affluence . . . Finally, the prophets call us to be advocates, lobbyists for those who are powerless in our time." [9]

With testimonies like these, it is difficult to dismiss the relevance of these prophets to contemporary US moral–political issues.

God's Stewards of All Life Relationships

It may seem strange to some Christians to make a biblical concept of humans as God's stewards one of a few theological cornerstones for framing a discussion on how to relate biblical texts to major issues in the news. However, this should not be that surprising if recognized that traditionally stewardship has been thought of as a "means to an end" seasonal program in churches that are primarily focused on financing church organizational operations. This traditional view has been seriously challenged in recent decades.

7. Bright, *The Kingdom of God*, 67. *Bibliography*

8. Bruggemann, *The Journey to the Common Good*, 119, *Bibliography*

9. Limburg, *The Prophets and the Powerless*, 98. *Bibliography*

A steward may be broadly defined as anyone who administers anything as an agent of another. Theologically, however, it is a holistic understanding of an accountability relationship to God as Creator–owner. Even the Christological focus of the New Testament should not neglect the theological assumption that Jesus Christ is presented in the New Testament not in the role as owner, but as the authentic and preeminent steward: 'all are yours, and you are Christ's and Christ is God's.'" (1 Cor. 3:22–23)[10] The notion of being a steward was known in the Old Testament as early as the history of Abraham's descendants ending up slaves in Egypt.

Abuse of power as bad stewardship

As recorded in the book of Genesis, when Joseph arrived in Egypt the pharaoh was having bad dreams about possible future wheat scarcity that caused him great anxiety. Joseph was asked to interpret one of these dreams and he predicted a seven-year severe famine. Pharaoh responded to this prophecy by making Joseph his chief steward in storing up wheat for a famine. But instead of using this accumulated wheat for the common good of all his subjects, this pharaoh exploited those in need to increase the number and the work-severity of his slaves. These included the people of Israel.

Walter Bruggemann, again in his book, *Journey to the Common Good*, outlines how slavery developed under anxious fearful Pharaohs, "by the manipulation of the economy in the interest of a concentration of wealth and power for the few at the expense of the community . . . *Those who are living in anxiety and fear, most explicitly of scarcity, have no time or energy for the common good.*" [11] The book of Genesis tells of this process with stark objectivity as Joseph carried out a policy driven by Pharaoh's bad dreams about scarcity. In order to keep receiving enough food, the people first used up all their money, and then their cattle, then their lands, and finally they gave themselves up into slavery. (Genesis 47:13–21) This short account can be seen as a good example of bad governmental moral stewardship that has repeatedly happened in history.

The Israelites were victims of this exploitative ruthlessness and God heard their prayers. God objected to such abuse of power. Through Moses, God freed them from this slavery. One of the admonition themes that clearly defined the biblical understanding of God's people as stewards

10. Hall, *The Steward*, 26, 42–43. *Bibliography*

11. Bruggemann, *The Journey to the Common Good*, 6–7. *Bibliography*

rather than ultimate owners is Deuteronomy 8:17: "Beware lest you say in your heart, 'My power and the power of my right hand have gotten me this wealth. You shall remember the Lord your God for it is he who gives you power to get wealth that he may confirm his covenant, which he swore to your father s at this day. But if you forget your God and go after other gods and serve them, you shall surely die."

The timeless message is simple: If we act as if what we have title to is ours to do with as we please rather than something we are responsible to God for, our long-term well-being and that of our society are in jeopardy.

Owner vs. God's stewards and witnesses

As noted in the previous section on the prophets, Moses' descendants eventually prospered in the united clans and kingdoms under David and Solomon. But this prosperity brought decadence, division, judgment, and exile.

Jesus came several centuries later and identified himself as more in the line of the prophets rather than other leadership groups of his time. In his teaching, Jesus did not ignore the issues the that prophets cited. Jesus summarized the concept of being stewards with admonitions such as, "Where your treasure is, so will your heart be also." In Matthew 6:22 this assertion is followed with warnings to not store up treasures on earth (the temporal kingdom) where all things decay. Instead, Jesus admonished followers to lay up spiritual treasures in the eternal kingdom, which it is "your Father's good pleasure to give you." In these words, the link between the temporal and the eternal is clear. In the context of the entire biblical proclamation, the location of one's treasure has both temporal and eternal implications. The Christian lives in two realms with responsibility in both.

Jesus explicitly used the concept of steward without using the word in his teaching. For example, "It shall be like a man going on a journey who turned his property over to his servants while he was gone." The servants had some discretion in management but were accountable for how they managed everything in reporting to the "owner" when he returned.

The "man going on a journey" motif of an owner leaving his affairs with someone as a steward was used in six different parables. In some of the parables, it referred to money and property but also referred to how those left in charge treated other persons. The biblical concept of a steward is holistic, involving all of life, not something involving only money matters. God the Creator remains owner of all creation, and all humans are stewards held accountable whether or not they sign on as citizens in the invisible realm of the Kingdom of God. If they do sign on, it should be as counter-cultural witnesses against corruption and abuse of power in the kingdoms of this world.

Over 100 years ago, the highly respected Christian historian Adolph van Harnack gave special emphasis to the "political" nature of Jesus' witness:

> What the political church wants . . . is to rule, to get ahold of men's souls and bodies, consciences and worldly goods. What political parties want is the same; and when the heads of these parties set themselves up as popular leaders, a terrorism is developed which is often worse than the fear of royal despots. It was not otherwise in Jesus' day. The priests and the Pharisees held the nation in bondage and murdered its soul. For this unconstituted "authority" Jesus showed an emancipating disrespect. He never tired of attacking it—nay, in his struggle with it he roused himself to a state of holy indignation—of exposing its wolfish nature and hypocrisy, and declaring that its day of judgment was at hand. In whatever domain it had any warrant to act, Jesus accepted it: "Go and show yourselves to the priests" . . . To these spiritual "authorities," then, he filled his disciples with a holy want of respect. [12]

In the New Testament epistles, the book of Acts, and in the first three centuries of the Christian church, Christians were a non-violent, persecuted minority. And from what little we know, this made every aspect of their life relationships a matter of management with Christ at the center. The Jesus model was pacifist in standing against violence by non-violent means, but activist in speaking truth to power about justice vs. mercy issues. This stance carries risks. Some think this "activist" through his words is at least part of what made Jesus "crucifiable."

It is not clear how much this witness accountability relates to heaven vs. hell distinctions vs. this-world consequences. But it is hard to escape the conclusion that deliberate bad stewardship could have definite negative consequences in the temporal realm.

Power corrupts

The early church life-style changed in 330 CE when Constantine made Christianity the official religion of the Roman Empire. Christianity became

---

12. Harnack, *What is Christianity?* Reference cited in Keck, 25. *Bibliography*

"established." The result of Constantine's action was that Church and State became mixed into almost one entity in which princes became bishops or vice versa—the so-called "Holy Roman Empire" that lasted into the middle ages.

Wars, crusades, inquisitions, imperial conquest and even ethnic cleansings followed, most carried forward in the name of Christianity. Wars may be inevitable. But it is hard to reconcile justifying wars in the name of what Jesus taught. Luther would later label such actions a degradation of a biblical theology of the cross into a human–engineered theology of glory.

Another change in the ancient church after Constantine was that the biblical concept of an honored role of believers as God's stewards became for most practical purposes buried. Life became a negative toil on the way to heaven. The notion that the message contained the ingredients for making life better in this life was at least partly discounted.

The Reformation made things somewhat better. Luther's catechism explained the Ten Commandments in their positive meanings for this life, not just in the negative "Thou shall nots." But before long, most Catholic and Protestant churches in Europe became culturally, even if not always politically, "established" (tax supported). Belief continued to mean an assent to doctrine associated with "cultural" Christian festivals. Ethics also had become largely individual morality of "sins" (mostly sexual), whereas serving as constructive critics of government and society in the prophetic tradition seemed to not count. A few voices such as the Danish theologian Kierkegaard criticized what they considered had become a caricature of real faith.

Ethics: one vs two sphere

In the centuries following the Reformation, the Christian moral life became more and more divided into secular vs. sacred realms. As already noted in chapter 1, Dietrich Bonhoeffer called this an inferior "two sphere" (sacred/ secular) mentality that corrupted ethics into two spheres rather than a biblically constant effort to work toward a biblical "one sphere" holistic ethic of life that called for the same ethic in church and society. In Bonhoeffer's words:

> The main understanding of ethical thought has become the conception of a juxtaposition and conflict of two spheres, the one divine, holy, supernatural and Christian, and the other worldly,

34

profane, natural and un-Christian . . . This division of the total
reality into a sacred and profane sphere . . . creates the possibility of existence in one of two of these spheres which can claim
autonomy for itself in dealing with the other sphere . . . he seeks
Christ without the world or the world without Christ. [13]

The visible- temporal realm as distinct from the invisible- spiritual
part of reality is not limited to a biblical concept. Concepts of fairness, justice, and love, or the good, the true, and the beautiful are in the invisible
realm and are frequently referred to in all areas of life with no reference
to the Bible. Bonhoeffer's claim is that this two–realm distinction of reality does not warrant a parallel double standard of ethics with a different
code in each realm. Such moral codes undermine any society where it is
significantly operative, often by one code discounting the other. The Bible-
newspaper discipline attempts a one–sphere ethic that fits comfortably with
a holistic biblical stewardship concept. [14]

In recent decades, theologians such as Douglas John Hall noted that
the traditional view of stewardship was not consistent with the Bible or with
what is known about the practice of Christians in the first three centuries of
the church. Most of American life was lived as if in a realm of secular ethics
separated from the spiritual concept of living as God's stewards. It was in
this secular realm that issues of industrialization and economic theories
such as free market capitalism were debated and formulated. The "evil"
atheistic nature of Communism gave free market capitalism an image of
being at least more Christian. That is, if and when it was related to biblical
theology at all. Professor Hall's book, *The Steward: a symbol come of age*,
documented this reality. Hall notes:

Far from standing for a basic orientation to the world or even a
major image of the life and work of the church, stewardship is regarded as a sort of optional ethic for the enthusiastic churchman
or woman . . . Rarely does one encounter Christians for whom the
metaphor represents a kind of summing up of the meaning of the
Christian life. It is just possible that today one would be able to
find more people outside the churches who are beginning to think
of stewardship in holistic terms than one finds inside them . . . . In
short, stewardship should no longer be concerned with matters—
including religious matters—only on the periphery of existence;
it belongs to the essence of things. It is for us today very close to

13. Bonhoeffer, *Ethics*, 196–197, *Bibliography*
14. Ibid., 198–207.

what the prophets and apostles meant by the Word of God. For the call to responsible stewardship encounters us precisely at the heart of our present-day dilemma and impasse. [15]

Professor Hall "pushed the envelope" of this holistic sense of stewardship ethics into the political sphere, which at times linked being holistic stewards to being theologians of the cross. The writings of biblical scholars like Hall encouraged me to attempt opinions with a relevant biblical reference, whether or not this connection was always stated.

Two Bible verses from Paul appropriately sum up the idea of becoming God's holistic stewards with a one-sphere ethic:

"This is how one should regard us, as servants of Christ and stewards of the mysteries of God. Moreover, it is required of stewards that they be trustworthy." (1 Cor. 4:1–2)

"For who sees anything different in you? What have you that you did not receive? If you received it, why do you boast as if it were not a gift?" (I Cor. 4:7)

We Live in Two Realms

In Karl Barth's Bible–newspaper metaphor relationship to my newspaper experience, the Bible implicitly represents one realm of reality, and the news media represents another. In some sense this division is artificial because both make up a complete reality and the process seeks a unity in more than one way. Neither the media nor earthly kingdoms should be regarded as subversive forces because both are important to civil societies, especially democratic ones. Both realms engaged with the other are better than if sharply separated. Christians are called into the material world, and thus are living simultaneously in the two realms, whether choosing to be activists in either, both, or neither. Christians are "in" the worldly kingdoms but not "of" them. This section attempts to augment this understanding using insights from different theologians, most of whom have already been cited on other topics.

Thinking of two-order living is not as explicitly helpful in making biblical judgments of newsworthy issues as the first three themes are. Evaluation of issues in the dynamics of two realms is more subjective than thinking in the frameworks of the other themes. But for me the concept

15. Hall, *The Steward*, 15, 95. *Bibliography*

helps keep matters in perspective by recognizing the difference between the finite–temporal, and the infinite–eternal. It also helps distinguish the difference between material and spiritual realities.

The two–realm understanding has been important to me because I cannot remember a time that I did not sense a spiritual realm, even from the age that theologian Marcus Borg calls that of "pre-critical naiveté." My faith experience has not included some sudden "conversion," but rather a persistent awareness of an invisible dimension where importance of true vs. false, right vs. wrong, good vs. bad, love vs. hate, justice vs. injustice and other invisible realities are experienced.

As suggested in the Introduction, all my life I have figuratively "ascended" in the spiritual realm for reflection and nourishment when I attend church on Sundays, and then "descend" into world relationships during the week. In this I am not that different from many, if not most, Christians.

This chapter briefly explores the views of four theologians on these two realms to help establish their reality and relationships.

John Bright: The Kingdom of God

One of the biblical accounts most relevant to questions of biblical morality related to contemporary socio–political issues has already been noted—that of the rise of the Davidic kingdom to fulfillment of the promised land, "filled with milk and honey."

The main point to note here is that many Israelites came to understand the notion of living together under God in a "kingdom" came largely from memories and records handed down from the Davidic kingdom. This perception helped fuel the hope that a military–style messiah similar to David might show up. But even though that hope wasn't realized, the idea of God as king served metaphorically for the first Jewish Christians to resonate with Jesus' proclamation of the "Kingdom of God," transitioned into an invisible kingdom "not of this world."

In relationship to this history, Bright defines God as "a moral being who controls nature and history, and in them reveals his righteous will and summons men to obey it." Bright's definition of the Kingdom of God is, "The whole notion of the rule of God over his people, and the vindication of that people in glory at the end of history." [16] This idea began with the de-

16. Bright, *The Kingdom of God*, 18. *Bibliography*

scendants of Abraham who "did not believe merely that a God existed, but also that this God had, in a historical act, entered into a covenant with her, and made her his people." [17] This was a covenant of grace, with the Exodus history of deliverance a primary expression of it.

The Kingdom of God phrase was one of the most frequent used by Jesus as recorded in the gospels. Jesus used the term 38 times in the Gospel of Matthew, 14 times in Mark, 32 times in Luke, and twice in John. According to Bright, Jesus as the Christ came "to give a radical reorientation to existing morality." This was orientation to the person of Jesus the Christ. This was the "new thing" spoken of by the prophets. A specific biblical "new thing" was that "the Kingdom of God had become also the Kingdom of Christ." [18]

But this new thing was not an earthly political kingdom. The kingdom of God was "at hand," not only something to wait for in the hereafter. Although the gospel summons is to obedience in certain tasks, its summons is also to a *destiny* granted by grace. It is to be a people over whom God rules, who exhibit the righteousness of God's kingdom before the world. Christian conduct is to reflect the fact she (the church) is a people set apart to God. Neither any earthly kingdom nor any church can be equated with the biblical notion of the Kingdom of God.

According to Bright, individual to individual conduct is important, but only part of the response expected of Christians. How Christian groups get along with different groups is also important, from those of small size to nation states:

> We have learned that we have not to do with sins: a list of the more obvious misdemeanors which a good man doesn't commit anyhow, or for which he may by force of will desist. We have to do with the total and corporate failure in the realm of righteousness, a failure that places a world of justice and peace forever beyond his grasp as if it were some lost Eden guarded by a cherub's flaming sword . . . History is a judgment, and it is civilization that is judged . . . This judgment hangs over us; we do not know how to save ourselves from it, frantically though we try. And it is to this context of desperation that the Church today speaks. Speaks, and proclaims her gospel . . . Let men then make decision for this New Age by repentance and baptism for the remission of sins! [19]

17. Ibid., 26.
18. Ibid., 197.
19. Ibid., 247.

The above assertion does not mean that human effort can bring on utopia or a full realization of "heaven on earth." But a righteous human response can bring improvements that have some approximations of what God intended, and which may prevent some of the worst nightmares humans can collectively create for themselves. In Bright's terms, the destiny that gives Christians the courage to collectively speak and act against "corporate failures in the realm of righteousness" is belief in the rule of God over his people, and its ultimate vindication.

Corporate failures need corporate repair, so Bright speaks also to societal lapses. For example:

> To pray, "Thy Kingdom Come," is to pray precisely that the rule of God triumph everywhere. It is a prayer that cannot be prayed while we declare that there are areas of life where the will of Christ will not rule, but our ancient prejudice does. The Church is to exhibit the righteousness of Christ not only in private morality but also in all matters of human relations. *The church which "sticks to the gospel" and utters no word of judgment or exhortation to society's sin, is no church, and what is worse, is preaching an incomplete gospel.* The Kingdom of God is supreme over the earthly order and by its righteousness pronounces judgment and summons to penitence" (italic emphasis added). [20]

After these strong admonitions about the church moving beyond personal morality into the realm of all human relationships, some pages later Bright places them in the context of the theology of the cross:

> We must stand before that cross, which is, and must remain, our redemption . . . But we must rid ourselves of clichés. The cross is no doctrinal abstraction to which a man may give credence passively, as though there were some magic in that . . . On the contrary, we lay hold on something essential, and essentially sharable, in the cross of Christ. Before the cross was erected there was another, inner crucifixion whereby that crucifixion was accepted. It took place when the very righteousness of God surrendered itself without limits to serve the purpose of God in history. This, then, is our cross: our total surrender to the Kingdom of God . . . No longer will we cry: spare me; spare my church; spare my country! But: use me, use my church' use my country—to the utmost for thy purposes which are right and good![21]

20. Ibid., 263.
21. Ibid., 270–271.

Paul Tillich: Living in Two Orders

Paul Tillich was one of the great theologians of the last century. In a book of fifteen of his sermons, one is titled. "We live in two orders."[22] One order is the historical order, that of human history. What Tillich emphasizes in the difference between the two orders is the difference between human finiteness and something that is eternal. Like the life of every human that grows, matures, and dies, so go all the collective human enterprises, no matter how seemingly great or small. The other order is the eternal order, ordered by the God that created the world that the temporal historical order that humanity lives in.

The text used for Tillich's sermon is the 40th chapter of what has been designated Second Isaiah. It was written for the exiles in Babylon, their nation destroyed with the exiles separated from their homeland. This is the world of sin and punishment that follows. The exiles are where they are for failing to live up to the covenant their forbearers were called to.

But pretentiously the prophet calls out, "Comfort ye, comfort ye, my people says your God . . . Speak comfortably to Jerusalem and cry unto her that her warfare is accomplished, that her iniquity is pardoned." (Isaiah 40:1–2) From the prophet's lips and pen, words of darkness and light, praise and lament, follow each other like the rising and falling waves in a turbulent ocean. Words of the eternal realm break into the temporal that something new is happening: "He shall feed his flock like a shepherd . . . " The exiles and their children will return to Jerusalem.

This cycling of history is because of what the Bible calls sin and punishment, a tragic flaw that ordains finiteness. Greatness can be found in history, even nations that manifest a certain amount of righteousness. There are judges, and even just judges. There are states and constitutions that even grant some amount of freedom and equality. But they are all subject to the tragic law of self-destruction. Humans become proud of even their goodness, such that it undermines its own longevity. Such is "the arrogance of our rationalism and the narrowness of our moralism."

To this tragic reality the prophet speaks a message of hope that is, however, by human standards paradoxical. The prophet points to the power that created the universe, but he does not speak of some supernatural cataclysm that will set things right. Instead he speaks of a mysterious "suffering servant." This is a clue to the alternative reality that is the foundation of the

---

22. Tillich, *The Shaking of the Foundations*, 12. *Bibliography*

"other order," where "the word of the Lord will stand forever." This eternal order is different and separate from the historical order, but humans can participate in it. It is such that makes humans that participate always in it always dissatisfied with what they accomplish, reducing the risk of pretentious arrogance. But this "participation in the infinite" touches something in the depth of the soul that knows that realm is real. The paradoxical image of the crucified suffering servant opens the door to participation in two orders, not only a tragic one. His is a message twenty-first century Americans should ponder.

Reinhold Niebuhr: "The Kingdom not of This World"

Another of the last century's greatest theologians was an American, Reinhold Niebuhr. A book of his sermons, *Beyond Tragedy,* was first published in 1937. One of these sermons was titled, "The Kingdom Not of this World," based on Jesus' response to Pilate: "My kingdom is not of this world." (John 18;36) This confrontation, according to Niebuhr, reflected an ageless drama of prophetic voices of another realm standing before rulers of a worldly order who are attempting to judge the truth-tellers. Typical of this world's rulers, Pilate was only interested in how much his power was threatened by the person brought before him. When Jesus said that his kingdom was not of this world, Pilate relaxed: "I find no crime in him."[23]

In a different circumstance, Pilate might have offered Jesus a position of auxiliary power. Then Jesus would have been an instrument of worldly power. Many a priest in history has succumbed to such invitations. Most rulers considered a good priest to be one who persuades his people that their primary concerns should be with another world. Bad rulers think that bad priests in terms of their agenda are those that transmute religion into political discontent over injustices.

In witnessing to this clash of kingdoms, Jesus told Pilate that his was a kingdom of truth: "To this end I was born, and to this end came I into the world to bear witness to the truth." To this Pilate responded with the contemptuous sneer, "What is truth?" (John 18:38) This central truth that Jesus testified to, yet to be more fully revealed, was that the world was alienated from its true character by sin. Injustices abound.

This truth Jesus bears witness to lies in the *moral* character of the Kingdom not of this world. Yet Jesus' Kingdom is in the world and impinging

---

23. Niebuhr, *Beyond Tragedy*, 271. *Bibliography*

upon every decision every human ever makes. Men may be greedy, but even in their own acts, most people know that greed is wrong. Apostles of greed such as Ayn Rand are able to sell greed as an important ingredient of their philosophy in the world, some at the same time claiming to be a part of the Kingdom of God. In so doing, they are insurrectionists in the Kingdom not of this world, undermining the moral foundations and health of the very kingdoms that they rule: "the grass withers." (Isaiah 40:7)

Reference will be made to Reinhold Niebuhr in Chapter 3 in an opinion I wrote regarding refugees examined under Niebuhr's concept of *Moral Man and Immoral Society*—the title of one of his better-known books.[24] This phrase designates a reality that as individuals, most persons recognize a moral need for compassion and generosity toward others in need and some act on it in extraordinary ways. But when individuals band together in likeminded groups, the group ego mentality usually diminishes their moral capacities compared to what they would do as individuals. This is especially true as against other groups with whom they have competitive relationships. The most selfish expressions (and hypocrisies) are often in nation states.

One of Niebuhr's typical expressions of this theme is, "As individuals, men believe they ought to love and serve each other and establish justice between each other. As racial, economic, and national groups, they take for themselves whatever their power can command."[25] Because of inevitable conflicts of interest, it is often necessary to form groups to stand against others who abuse power. Such opposition represents moral action. The ultimate failure of the "soft power" compromise between coercive and persuasive approaches occurs when the issues end in resorting to war, where moral blindness becomes most evident. From a biblical perspective, wars are not occasions for glorifying the need for killing.

Dietrich Bonhoeffer: Church and State

In his unfinished *Ethics*, Dietrich Bonhoeffer devoted about twenty pages to a section titled, "State and Church," which provides yet another example of how the Kingdom not of the world engages the kingdoms of this world. In the first paragraph, Bonhoeffer starts with this premise: "Government is the power that creates and maintains order . . . government is divinely

24. Niebuhr, *Moral Man and Immoral Society. Bibliography*
25. Ibid., 9.

ordained authority to exercise worldly dominion by divine right . . . It can only be understood [properly] from above"[26]

This "divinely ordained authority" understanding applies whether or not any government or ruler accepts the Bible as having any relevance. Thus, Jesus told Pilate, "You would not have your authority over me unless it were given from above." God used the nations of Assyria, Babylon and Persia to historically subdue and then release some of the people who had turned their backs on God. These biblically historical events demonstrate that in some sense, all nations are "under God."

Thus in Bonhoeffer's view, governments are judged by God, whether or not they claim some biblical relationship, or whatever percentage of their citizens are members of a given religion. What is primarily required of governments is "not some Christian action, but an action that does not exclude Christ." For governments that claim no biblical identity, a judgment by eternal standards may relate to congruity with the second able of the Ten Commandments. Some actions by groups or nations that claim less Christian identity than others may be more moral than some that claim to be "Christian." Thus, we have Martin Luther's alleged comment: "I would rather be ruled by a competent Turk (in those days meaning a Muslim) than an incompetent Christian."

After defining the nature of the state, Bonhoeffer turns to the political responsibility of the church: "It is part of the Church's office of guardianship that she should call sin by its name and that she should warn men against sin; for righteousness exalts a nation, but sin is perdition for the people." (Proverbs 14:34) "If the Church did not do this, she would be incurring part of the guilt for the blood of the wicked.[27]

Bonhoeffer defines some of the characteristics of a state needed to fulfill this role in relationship to the Church. One thing governments should not do, is help religions promulgate their doctrines. Rather they are to set conditions that allow religious organizations to function and thrive. This would be consistent with the First Amendment of the US Constitution. But in turning to what the Church in Germany had been doing in its responsibilities to the state, Bonhoeffer concluded:

> The Church has so far failed to master the social, economic, political sexual, and educational problems. The dogmatically correct delivery of the Christian proclamation is not enough; nor are

26. Bonhoeffer, *Ethics*, 332. *Bibliography*

27. Ibid., 350.

general ethical principles; what is needed is concrete instruction in the concrete situation . . . In brief, the Church must offer solutions for the unsolved problems of the world, and thereby fulfill her mission and restore her authority.[28]

But at the same time, Bonhoeffer suggests that without a biblical proclamation that transforms citizens into a higher moral plain than pure self-interest, expertise in the so-called secular realm of knowledge may have limited effectiveness.

Christ "affirms reality," according to Bonhoeffer, which means the Christian should strongly respect what science comes to consensus about regarding reality of the natural world.[29] The real is related to what is true because depictions with something counterfeit is to make a false statement. If there is intent to deceive, this makes the statement a lie, a breach of the eighth commandment. The issue is moral. Bonhoeffer wrote:

> The question here is whether within the field of Christian ethics any assertions may be made with regard to worldly institutions and conditions, e.g. the state, economics or science, i.e. or whether in fact these things are ethically neutral . . . *Has the church merely to gather up those who the wheel has crushed or has she to prevent the wheel from crushing them?* (italics added).[30]

This brings us back to the statement quoted in the introduction of this book about the wheels that crush. The above italicized words were written sometime between 1939 and 1943. I have not researched to find out when Bonhoeffer learned about the worst of what was happening to Jewish people in Germany. But the "crushing wheel" metaphor likely refers to what was happening to the Jewish people, and even if not, it is on target for what happened. It certainly points to the reality of what can happen if the Church and other institutions choose only to try to aid those crushed by the wheels of injustice, and do not act early enough to stop bad trends from getting beyond control.

28. Ibid., 354.
29. Ibid., 85.
30. Ibid., 321.

Two Kingdom Summary

The two-kingdom or two-realm concept of human reality may seem so basic to the biblical message that some might say that "it goes without saying." But one might then ask what the evidence is that most persons, or most Christians, live as if they exist in two realms rather than just one. The answer is not easy.

The two-realm pairing extends the Bible-Newspaper metaphor from personal engagement of issues into the cosmic moral realm of what the Bible considers the "eternal." It is where, if we choose, live touching the eternal while living in the temporal. The biblical message posits that beyond the visible, audible, and tactile experience of life there is an invisible realm with effects similar to the scientific laws of gravity, inertia, and electromagnetism. Although unseen, their effects can be observed, and the realities are best not ignored. Jesus told Nicodemus, "Do not marvel that I told you 'You must be born anew.' The wind blows where it wills and you hear the sound of it, but you do not know from whence it comes or whither it goes; so it is of everyone who is born of the Spirit." (John 3:7–8) It is within this realm that concepts such as truth, love, justice, and fairness are best understood.

A cautionary note to insert here is that the two-realm reality message does not presume a different moral code for the different realms. In fact, as Bonhoeffer emphasized and has been noted here, there should not be one ethic for the so-called sacred realm and another for the secular or profane. That is the world's way of double standards. The world of the Spirit posits one ethic. The Church occupies a space in that it has a place for worship and teaching, and in that space respect and decent language are usually found. But this separation does not mean that insults, locker room talk, and cheating are acceptable outside of that space. God in Christ reconciled the whole world, and those who claim reconciliation should show it.

The main point of relevance of living in two realms for the subject categories of this book is that most major issues have a significant moral dimension. That dimension is in the moral–spiritual–eternal realm that should engage the temporal to achieve optimum solutions of unity. This is not easy, and the task is made especially difficult if there is denial of ethical realities. Biblically this applies, whether for health care, global warming, gun violence, refugees, wealth disparity, foreign policy, or many other issues.

Who is Ayn Rand?

There are two important reasons to understand who Ayn Rand was. First, as noted in the Introduction, Ayn Rand is not a Christian theologian. In fact, she was an avowed atheist. Rand represents the polar opposite of ethics derived from the Bible, especially on economic issues. Second, Rand has been recognized and praised by many US politicians, and many who know little of her espouse policies that fit closely to hers.

Rand was a Russian-born woman whose 1957 novel, *Atlas Shrugged*, so increased in popularity that for years it was second only to the Bible in books read annually in the US. In it Rand promotes her economic philosophy. In 2010, *Christianity Today* published an article about Rand titled, "Goddess of the Great Recession." This was authored by Gary Moore, a financial professional with a theological degree. "Goddess" referred to the reverence ascribed openly to her economic philosophy by some prominent politicians, and practiced by many others. [31]

Atlas Shrugged

The story in *Atlas Shrugged* primarily involves dynamics among a number of U.S. corporate leaders in heavy industries such as railroad, mining, steel, oil, and aircraft. As the nation slips into a severe economic downturn, a blame game debate ensues, which pits the corporate leader "makers" against the working class "parasite moochers" and "looters." The moochers are portrayed as both envious and unappreciative of the "Atlas" type corporate leaders who allegedly uphold the economy and well-being of everyone else. The plot peaks when, in a nationally broadcast radio address, the leader of a large group of corporate leaders surprisingly announces that most critical corporate business enterprises are on strike, effectively shutting down the economy. This address summarizes Ayn Rand's ultraconservative political and economic philosophy, for which she prefers the title, "Objectivism."

It is impossible to easily summarize this 57-page chapter, let alone the whole book. But a short summary is that the Rand view divides all persons into enterprising worthy vs. the lazy citizens that need to be motivated. [32] The primary message as I read it is that the two groups that most inhibit optimal capitalistic economics are governments and religion of any kind.

31. Moore, "Ayn Rand, Goddess of the Great Recession," 37–40

32. Rand, *Atlas Shrugged*, 923–90. *Bibliography*

Some observers consider the genius of this book to be the way Rand made business leaders to appears victims rather than selfish victimizers despite assertions such as, "We are on strike against those who believe that one man must exist primarily for the sake of another."

A few quotations are representative of Rand's philosophy: "Government should make no law abridging the freedom of production and trade." The recommended personal oath for economic success is: "I swear by my life and my love of it that I will never live for the sake of another man, nor ask another man to live for mine . . . We are on strike against unearned rewards and unrewarded duties . . . against your mystic (Christian) teachings that morality is a code of behavior imposed on you by a whim of a supernatural power, to serve God's purpose or your neighbor's welfare, to please an authority beyond the grave . . . If you saw Atlas struggling to keep the world up, what would you tell him to do?" Answer: Shrug critics off. In Rand's novel, this is accomplished by a strike by corporate leaders.

First published in 1957, this novel has frequently polled as a second favorite only to the Bible in influencing U.S. thinking—although it is manifestly anti-biblical. Religious morality produces individual and societal weakness, agnostic disciplined selfish reasoning produces strength. The connection to the 2008 "worst recession" in U.S. history is related by some analysts to the many noted political figures that testify to Rand's positive influence on their personal views.

Rand advocates

Wikipedia lists 35 Rand admirers and promoters. These include Martin Anderson (President Reagan's Sec. of the Treasury), former Fed Chairman Allan Greenspan, Glenn Beck, Sen. Rand Paul, Rep. Paul Ryan, Justice Clarence Thomas, and Senator Ted Cruz. For most economists, the validity of this "rational selfishness" economic philosophy is far from validated. But beyond this, for anyone who claims to take biblical theology seriously, some attention should be focused on the judgment of how blatantly anti-biblical this popular economic philosophy is. The noted Lutheran theologian Martin Marty observed, "Every line of the Bible is challenged, countered and dismissed by the 1,168 pages of *Atlas Shrugged*."[33]

Many current political statements in the press are typical Randian. Syndicated columnists Cal Thomas and Kathleen Parker have defended

33. Moore, *"Goddess of Meanness and Greed."* 28, 30

wealth disparity and castigated the lower classes for envying the rich. Sen. Ted Cruz read extensively from *Atlas Shrugged* during his 2013 shutdown-promoting filibuster. In 2011 House Speaker John Boehner quipped, "I think the job creators are on strike." More recently billionaires Sam Perkins and Tom Zell complained that that they were "victims" of a culture war, and they should be primarily emulated, not envied. Part of Rand's genius was to make wealthy corporate leaders appear as victims unappreciated by workers for their economic creativity.

One of the tightest associations of the Rand doctrine with the 2008 recession has been its link with Rand-admirer former Federal Reserve Chairman Alan Greenspan. The *Wall Street Journal* summarized one of Greenspan's congressional testimonies as: "My mistake was an expectation that the financial CEOs would adequately govern themselves . . . you might try more regulation." He acknowledged his admiration of Rand, in a November 2013 issue of *Foreign Affairs,* claiming that he did not see the 2008 meltdown coming. However, he didn't think it was fair to blame it on Rand.

For years US Representative Paul Ryan required all his staff to read *Atlas Shrugged,* until he introduced one of his economic bills that would have a severe negative impact on poor people. At that point, some Catholic organizations complained. Ryan, who is Roman Catholic, then distanced himself from Rand's atheism, but not from her economic philosophy.

While these unabashed Rand supporters in government may be relatively few, Rand's basic principles are closely in line with conservative economic ideology. No one knows the mind of another but votes on bills speak. Those who are for more tax cuts for the rich, don't think widening wealth disparity is bad, and vote against a higher minimum wage and decent health care access for all, are likely in Rand's camp, recognized or not.

Rand Syncretism

In 2010 I attended a conference sponsored by Luther Seminary on "Rethinking Stewardship." Gary Moore, the author noted at the beginning of this section was a speaker who explored Rand's direct influence on politics, and her indirect impact on Christian stewardship. Moore had a degree in political science, spent three decades on Wall Street, and had considered attending a seminary. However, he found that no seminaries taught anything about the ethics of money, so he founded his own Financial Seminary. All of the presentations of that conference were conveniently published in

Luther Seminary's theological journal, *Word and World*. [34] Some of Moore's main points are worth noting.

First, Moore's judgment was that American Christians have abandoned economic morality to the secular world. This is evidenced in part by some Christians espousing Rand concepts without citing their source in what Moore calls syncretism—a melding of opposite philosophies. For example, Pat Robertson has written, "The aim of free people everywhere has been to limit the scope of government in any way that they can."[35] Ralph Reed, a close associate of Robertson, wrote, "Traditionalist ends can be met through libertarian means."[36] These statements could be paraphrases from Ayn Rand's *Atlas Shrugged*. Such unholy alliances with Christianity and libertarianism are deemed unbiblical by most Christian thinkers who have studied the issue.

Second, Moore notes that many businessmen tell him they attend church and never hear discussion about the ethics of money. At the same time, "Tea Parties" are only economically focused, unconcerned about any social concerns. Even shortly after the credit and banking crisis in 2009 the *Wall Street Journal* published a major article entitled "Greed is Good," defending odious CEO compensation even though it reported that in 2006 the richest one percent received the highest percent of income since before the Great Depression.[37]

Third, some in the political sphere think it is okay for Christians to both carry the economic burden of caring for the poor while espousing Rand methods if most of their wealth is given away before death.[38] But few of the Ken Lays of the world do this, and conservative efforts always seem to be in the direction of reducing inheritance taxes. If laws permit more and more wealth disparity, shouldn't Christians resist that trend as a means of combating poverty? The great Jewish philosopher Maimonides wrote that it is more righteous to prevent poverty than to address poverty through charity.

In summary, a significant number of theologians consider a syncretism of Rand with Christianity by some American Christians to be a corrupted theology of the cross—a perverse theology of glory. Such theologies

34. Ibid., 28, 30.

35 Robertson, *The New Millennium*, 13. *Bibliography*

36. Reed, "Conservative Coalition Holds Firm," A–14.

37. *Wall Street Journal* editorial, "Greed is Good," W1.

38. Meeks, *The Doctrine of God*, 30. *Bibliography*

risk a path leading to using coercive and even violent measures to promote or defend Christianity, inconsistent with biblical norms. Such melding of Christian doctrine with secular philosophies might qualify for what Karl Barth calls bad religion, or even superstition. In any case, these ideologies may not bode well for the health of the nation.

Chapter 2 Summary

Martin Luther's understanding of the theology of the cross, the moral indictments of the Old Testament prophets, the biblical understanding of humans as God's relational stewards, the two-realm concept of reality, and Ayn Rand's anti-spiritual philosophy frame an approach to relating the Bible to major moral issues of our time. These themes provide some foundation for search and selection of biblical texts more specific to specific subject categories in the news. These theological themes provide my broad context for the next chapter's review of the engagement of biblical texts more specific to the issues engaged in newspaper opinions.

CHAPTER 3

Engaging Bible and Newspaper

THE CROSS AS A symbol of the crucifixion of Jesus is the supporting center from which all else is usually related for most Christians. One of its primary meanings in Luther's understanding is the "soft power" of "The Word" distinguished from coercive "hard power" applied in much of life. As such, the Kingdom of God must be regarded to some degree always at odds with human institutions that must rely on hard power to govern. This does not mean that governments are evil, but their hard power nature should be regarded as a potentially dangerous force tempting officeholders and contending lobbyists toward abusing their power for selfish purposes. This misuse should be vigilantly guarded against.

Christians are called to stand as arm's length constructive critics of such power, no matter what country they live in. In the US, news outlets do this by vocational expectation in their editorial-opinion role under the First Amendment of the US Constitution. Churches could also organize to do the same, recognizing that neither they nor any government can achieve a status of being the Kingdom of God on earth. The status of congregations as a part of a "kingdom not of this world" could be persuasive in adding moral strength and longevity to any society that allows it. But for various reasons that will be later addressed, little dialogue on major issues occurs among Christians inside or outside of their congregations.

This chapter moves from related theological themes to reviews of responses I made to reader, editor, and journalist opinions. I always had a biblical framework in mind in writing opinions, but its relevance and explicit mention were variable. However, each subject category in this review begins with a "Bible in one hand" section that cites some biblical or theologically relevant sources. The second section in each subject category is titled, "With a newspaper in the other hand," in which highlights of opinions are briefly reviewed. Twenty-three of the opinions referenced with letter–number designations in this chapter are reprinted in Appendix B as originally published.

A. Biblical Interpretation

The Bible in One Hand

The biblical background for this Biblical interpretation section consists of all themes reviewed in chapter 2.

With a Newspaper in One Hand

Opinions placed in this Bible category were those only about theological issues, or that had primarily a biblical premise for a position on some issue in the news.

Messiah as myth

A pastor wrote an opinion stating that the claim that Jesus was the Messiah is not a myth. A science teacher responded to this essay, asserting that the pastor's claim was a myth because the original group of gospels from which four were canonized included multiple documents written by forgers, along with other allegations. The teacher noted that Albert Schweitzer, in his quest for the historical Jesus, found little of substance for the quest that was looking for a different Jesus than portrayed in the gospels.

I found weaknesses in the arguments on both sides, but my main conclusion was that neither opinion gave readers a clue about where they stood on the critical moral issues of the day. Making that connection would have revealed much more about their comparative moral authenticity than debating only about a disputed theological claim. (A–1)

Science vs. faith

Two letter opinions were critical of "agnostic science" as it related to biblical faith in determining what it means to "know" spiritual truths. (A–2,3) The false premise in both letters was the assumption that to "know" something as true or real in science uses the same criteria that theology uses in addressing knowledge in questions of faith. The two disciplines overlap but distinguishing the spiritual from the material and recognizing this distinction is a prerequisite for productive discussion. Science doesn't reject metaphorical or spiritual reality. It only claims such realities cannot be subjected to scientific methods like most natural world realities can.

Over the years a number of readers used a literalist interpretation of the Noah flood story to discredit scientific warnings about the harmful effects of global warming. In one letter this claim was based on God's promise that, "never again will all life be cut off by waters of the flood." (A-4) One problem with this assertion is that few, if any, scientists claim global warming will destroy "all life." The text also says nothing against the possibility of other means of destroying much of life (such as droughts or a nuclear holocaust), or use of other agents such as humankind.

Finally, most of the letters alleged that the reason God caused the flood was sin, which is not literally correct. The word "sin" is never used in the Noah account. The text includes the words, corrupted, wickedness, evil and, "the earth was filled with violence." (Genesis 6: 11–12) This substitution allows an interpreter to select a favorite sin but avoid others, such as gun violence.

A letter's thesis was that" God creates all wealth," which in one sense is true, but it omits the more basic biblical stewardship assertion that God created everything without which there would be nothing for mankind to use in creating wealth. (A-3) The important biblical assertion about wealth is that human title to something does not constitute true ownership. Furthermore, God's purpose in collective titles to property and goods includes societal management such that "there should be no poor in the land." Along with this, God opposes odious wealth disparity because it predisposes to covetous hostility and violence. Such reality is the polar opposite of God's call to be good stewards of all life relationships.

Fitting people for heaven.

A syndicated columnist opinion by Cal Thomas asserted that sermons that focus on worldly issues represent time taken from a pastor's calling, which is to preach a message that will "fit people for heaven." (A-12) This declaration is a direct antithesis to the Barth statements about Bible and

Newspaper, as well as Bonhoeffer's assertion about "wheels that crush." Jesus said "By their fruits you will know them."

Works of love and justice are evidence of gratitude for faith, not for merit. The Thomas advice is exactly what history notes bad rulers want from religion, which is to keep the focus on things other than peace and justice issues.

Nationally, many Christians, especially evangelicals, supported Donald Trump. But not all. As noted on page 7, of the most newsworthy examples was evangelical Tony Campolo who declared that the evangelicalism of old white men was in bad shape. The trip–wire for Campolo was Trump's election, which he claimed had ruined the building he once called home. This could also mean that a wider election loser in the election was all of American Christianity. (A–11)

A letter opinion advised that liberals should get back to the Bible. (A–14) This was presumably to be where conservatives were at the time. My response was to suggest that in many ways conservatives had also strayed from the Bible. An example was the Republican tilt away from the "soft power" importance of "the word" in state department diplomacy that should constantly work to prevent wars that require "hard power" military action. President Trump also preferred to end participation in the Iran Nuclear Treaty and unilaterally pulled the US out. Some conservatives seem to have what Bonhoeffer calls a "two-sphere" ethic (page 34) that precludes a holistic ethic that attempts to do everything it can to avoid violence before resorting to military action.

Smokescreen biblical morality

A reader opinion warned of God's judgment on American society for being lax on the "the sin of homosexuality." Syndicated columnist Cal Thomas also stated exactly this in an opinion, adding abortion. (A–10) Prioritizing sexuality issues his way is suspect for substituting this sin category for consideration of other moral lapses. This stance can serve as a psychological "cover." (Matthew 23:23) There is nothing wrong with formulating a position on these sexuality issues, but they can become part of a skewed ("two sphere") morality.

It seemed coincidentally poignant that the Thomas opinion appeared just before the "Access Hollywood" recordings of candidate Trump's "locker room" dialogue hit the news. It seemed timely to suggest that sexual harassment might be added to the sexuality sins that many think God might punish America for.

Summary

Opinion responses in the Bible category of this critique ranged from purely theological questions such as whether or not Jesus' claim to be the Messiah was a myth, to science vs. faith questions about whether one overruled the other. Some arguments claimed church leaders who engaged moral issues in the news were abandoning their main calling to "fit people for heaven" while others used biblical texts to support a view that one need not worry about global warming. As such, many opinions implicitly ignored prophetic indictments and biblical precedents to speak truth to power like Nathan did in confronting King David. In any case, opinions documented some inconsistent use of the Bible in addressing moral issues in the news, and how US Christianity is as rigidly divided against itself in parallel with what American political parties are. This reality diminishes the Bible's potential positive societal effects and the general credibility of Christianity.

B. Health Care

With Bible in One Hand

The four gospels have over forty references to Jesus' healings or his admonitions to his followers to do the same. For example: "And preach as you go, saying, 'The Kingdom of heaven is at hand. Heal the sick . . . cleanse the lepers . . . " (Matthew 10:7) In Matt. 25, Jesus was asked, "When did we see you sick and not come?" (B–1)A reasonable interpretation of the contemporary relevance of such texts is that for Jesus, preaching about the Kingdom without advocating equal access to health care compromises the gospel message, especially when most other advanced nations manage much better to meet this goal. Equal access policy is the moral foundation for the stance on health care in this section.

With Newspaper in One Hand

History of Health Care Reform

A pivotal event in U.S. health care history was the Clinton attempt to pass a universal single-payer health care plan in 1993 that failed. The historical importance of this attempt includes the means by which Republicans were able to block this plan with an alternative proposal. The conservative Heritage Foundation had formulated important elements of this plan a few years before, two of which were the universal mandates to buy insurance, and insurance exchanges. Senator John Chaffee (R-RI) authored the Republican bill, and later Governor Mitt Romney incorporated some of these features in his universal plan for Massachusetts. (B–2,3,12)

President Obama included the mandate and exchanges in the Affordable Care Act (ACA) proposal, erroneously thinking Republicans might support it because these elements were originally conservative ideas. But the conservative (Cruz /Tea Party) wing of the Republican Party would have none of it. Some observers claim that Republican objection to the ACA was not because of its stated objections of change of physician, "death panels," etc. Rather, opposition was because of fears that the ACA would work as well as Medicare and it would thereby significantly shift the electorate. (B–2)

Global Health System Comparisons

Most of the health care systems of the world come close to one of four different models: (1) single government payer to government–employed professionals (like England); (2) Single government payer to private providers (like Canada); (3) Employer and employee financing through insurance company payments to private providers (most insurance for persons under age 65 in the US); (4) out-of-pocket payment (Cambodia). The US has had a patchwork of all four models, represented in the above order by (1) the active military/VA; (2) Medicare/Medicaid; (3) employed adult citizens under age 65; (4) the uninsured US citizens. In the US, the insurance model (3) subsidizes the out-of-pocket uninsured group, especially for their emergency room care. The US insurance model also has the highest per capita administrative costs of the rest of the US and the world. (B–2)

T.R. Reid, who spent two years comprehensively studying world health systems concluded that, "A fundamental moral decision our country has made is that we have never decided to provide medical care for everybody who needs it."[1] Any criticism of the ACA that does not include credible alternatives is presumptively against universal coverage. Note that Reid labeled this a moral decision and judgment, with no reference to the Bible or any religion. Tens of thousands of US citizens are estimated to die every year because of the lack of basic insurance. (B–3,13, 15)

Free Market Medicine

A Republican argument against universal single payer universal health care insurance systems has been that insurance–mediated, free-market systems deliver the best quality care at the lowest cost. However, this proposition has been seriously challenged in both theory and from lack of evidence in practice. One such challenge came from Stanford Nobel laureate economist Kenneth Arrow back in 1963. Arrow's theory was in turn cited by Dr. Arnold Relman, the highly-respected internist and former editor of the *New England Journal of Medicine* in his book, *A Second Opinion*, published in 2007. [2] Relman summarized the Arrow thesis as, "The medical care system is set apart from other markets by some unique characteristics." These characteristics included:

- Patient demand for services is for conditions that at unpredictable times rise to an existential threat from life-threatening illness or injury.

- Buyer demand for services does not simply respond to the desires of buyers, but is primarily determined by the professional judgment of physicians regarding the needs of their patients.

- There are significant limitations on the entry of providers into the market resulting from the high costs and exacting standards of professional education.

- There is a relative insensitivity to costs and near absence of price competition (here referring to competition among providers, not insurers).

1. Reid, *The Healing of America*, 2. Bibliography
2. Relman, *A Second Opinion*, 22–24. Bibliography

- There is significant buyer uncertainty because of the great asymmetry of knowledge between provider and buyer for a particular service, and the consequences of action.

Arrow concluded that because of the way all these factors conspire, patients cannot independently decide what services they want in the same way consumers decide in the usual markets when shopping for what they want at the price they want to pay. Because a higher level of trust is required in medical care than in most venues, society must rely on non-market mechanisms such as educational standards and state licensure, rather than on the effects of the market and the choices of informed buyers. (B–6–8, 12, 17, 21)

Faulty Anti-health Reform Arguments

One of my views is that the U.S. health care system increases the risk of debt and bankruptcy for purchasers of health care, their employers, and eventually even the nation. But a typical opposing argument was that we should not tamper with the "best health care system in the world." (B–13) This statement could only come from someone who had good insurance coverage and good access to health care, quite unaware or indifferent to what it is to be like to need health insurance but not be able to afford it. But health care reform is not primarily to make what is good for the insured better. It is to get equal access to all.

Other letters misrepresented the ACA and single payer statistics from other countries such as Canada. (B–10–13,14) My wife and I were in Norway in 1988 and were told by a tour guide that then King Olaf was advised that it was time to have his cataracts removed. When asked about scheduling the surgery, he first asked how long the average Norwegian citizen had to wait. He was told six months, and he promptly asked to be scheduled in six months. We didn't attempt to get confirmation of that event, but if true it reflected a pride their citizens had in their leaders and systems in working for their common good. (B–15)

State and ACA Waiver Options

An alternative to a national health care system is a universal state system such as Governor Romney was able to get passed in Massachusetts. The

ACA had a waiver provision stating that, starting in 2017, individual states could modify the ACA, even to the point of replacing it with a universal state system. Minnesota developed such a plan and had its financial construct audited by an independent group, which found it to be sound. But Minnesota's Republican majority would not allow its introduction for possible adoption. I wrote several opinions in favor of it and visited a state legislator on its behalf. (B–6, 17, 18, 21)

Summary

The US health care system is a patchwork of different systems with big gaps and inefficiencies that inhibit millions of citizens from basic access to health care. This in turn impairs optimal morbidity and mortality statistics of the US in comparison with the twenty top democracies of the world. As noted and quoted before, this represents a comparative lack of moral intent and a consequent moral failing. The quickest and easiest fix for this system would be to expand Medicare single–payer to all citizens. One of the basic opposing arguments for decades has been that better free–market choice systems would improve quality and lower costs. This theory was discredited a half–century ago, without substantial evidence since that market forces work in health care like they do for other goods and services. This opposing ideology may be best understood as the effect of Ayn Rand's philosophy on the American political system (see pages 46–50). The biblical basis for adopting universal care is Jesus' many acts and admonitions to "heal the sick."

C. Homosexuality

With Bible in One Hand

Any biblically related inquiry into the reality of homosexuality should start with the fact that the words homosexual, heterosexual, and bisexual are not found in any ancient Hebrew or Greek texts of the Bible. These words were not invented until 1869, and in medical contexts designate the biological heritable (not chosen) variant spectrum of different attractions in the human race. Some modern translations of the Bible have inserted the word homosexual in some texts, although there is no good evidence that the modern variant spectrum was understood when the Bible was written. The original King James version of the Bible did not use the word homosexual, and no modern translations have the word heterosexual.

In modern understanding, this variation implies no significant differences in potential for living morally responsible and productive lives among persons assumed to have the normal variant (all groups in the spectrum have a small minority with pathological variants such as pedophilia). However, this also means that persons of all normal variants are at essentially equal risk of disabling mental disorders or acting irresponsibly. Many homosexual persons have suffered from depression and suicide due to societal hostility, especially in adolescence. Religious traditions have not been very helpful in reducing this risk.

Science is generally most concerned with distinguishing health vs. disease, and responsible vs. responsible behavior related to health, no matter what the sexual orientation. Religious tradition usually pre-judged anyone with same–sex attraction to be morally defective, no matter what other testing would show about the potential for morally responsible living.

The change in scientific understanding of sexuality has led to different interpretations of the biblical texts usually cited to judge homosexual persons negatively. This interpretation shift has been similar to those regarding the cosmos or whether or not epilepsy should be regarded as primarily due to demon possession. When the stories in Genesis 19 and Judges 19 (Sodom and Gibea) are compared, the most logical conclusion using modern evidence is that the rape-threatening men were heterosexuals using threatened same–sex rape as a first step to their preference for any women with the strangers.

Neither Jesus nor the Old Testament prophets included same-sex relationships in their sexuality prohibitions, but both Testaments included marital adultery. Jesus mentioned marital adultery, but only in relationship to remarriage after divorce, which in modern times is mostly ignored. These facts illustrate the selective bias of modern ethics related to Scripture, and they provide reasons for skeptics to have doubts about religious intellectual integrity.

A Princeton University theologian whose book reflects the modern scientific understanding is *A Time to Embrace.* [3] Its author, William Stacy Johnson, argues for equality in societal acceptance and legal same-sex unions. Johnson contends that "the most important verse in all of Scripture

---

3. Johnson, *A Time to Embrace,* 116–118. *Bibliography*

for the gay marriage debate" is Genesis 2:18: "It is not good for the human being to be alone." (C-1)

In the early 1990s I did some writing and speaking on the misrepresentations of the scientific understanding of homosexuality viewed when the ELCA was only attempting to adopt a new social statement. In a Lutheran theological journal, I made the following prediction about a widely held view same–sex attraction was a choice of rejecting intrinsic opposite-sex attraction.

> I predict that irrespective of what the ELCA social statement on sexuality eventually says about homosexuality, sexual orientation will continue to be more widely understood as an unintentional biological trait. This understanding will be influenced by scientific study results, more open personal testimony of respectable homosexual persons, and general ethical principles. If my prediction is true, this understanding of homosexuality with its ethical implications will have to be confronted later, if not now.[4]

Sixteen years later the ELCA in General Assembly voted to give homosexual persons equal membership standing, and a few years later the state of Minnesota voted to allow marriage.

With Newspaper in One Hand

A Paradigm Shift

Although the events in the American Psychiatric Association (APA) in the early 1970s did not make much news, big changes occurred. Mental health specialists in the 1960s were increasingly aware that the traditional treatment measures for homosexual persons with psychological problems were at best not working well, and at worst making some persons worse.

This was especially true for efforts to change sexual orientation. Since Freud, same–sex attraction was considered a mental disorder, diagnosed in medical records with a code just as diabetes or emphysema were. In 1973, the board of the APA recommended that this designation be dropped in favor of considering same-sex erotic attraction a normal variant.

The next year the APA adopted a non-discrimination resolution. The first part of it read:

---

4. Peterson, "Science and Scripture," 50.

> Whereas homosexuality per se implies no impairment in judg-
> ment, stability, or general social or vocational abilities, therefore
> be it resolved that the APA deplores all public and private discrim-
> ination against homosexuals in such areas as housing, public ac-
> commodation, and licensing, and declares that no burden of proof
> of such reliability or capacity be placed on homosexuals than that
> placed on other persons . . . [5]

In this simple but elegant resolution, science separated itself from religious tradition in the same way Galileo had done centuries before. Consensus medical science concluded that the psychological stresses of homosexual persons were mostly due to societal hostility and discrimination that gay and lesbian persons were subjected to, and not to anything in the condition per se. The most common condition in adolescents was is depression predisposing to suicide. A major source of this hostility came from traditional organized religion, but medical professional organizations did not mount a campaign against any religions. Occasionally scientific publications contained telling statements, such as one noting that the most problematic parents of homosexual adolescents were "authoritarian, conservative, and religious." [6]

Experience over time established the medical and ethical soundness of this decision in benefitting the mental health of homosexual persons. Many psychiatrists consider those 1973–74 actions to be ethically comparable to Rosa Parks' decision not to give up her bus seat. That may be an exaggeration, but it might be argued that it was one of the major paradigm shifts in health care history.

Controversy in the ELCA

Ongoing discussions about homosexuality in congregations and church assemblies began in the Evangelical Lutheran Church in America (ELCA) shortly after the merger that created the new church body in 1987. These produced resolutions urging more acceptance of gays and lesbians in synod and church-wide assemblies, but most did not pass.

During the early years of ELCA discussions, some readers and clergy opposed to the change published serious misrepresentations of the scientific understanding, and I responded to several both in the metro and

5. Krajeski, *Textbook of Homosexuality*, 18. *Bibliography*
6. Friedman and Downy, "Homosexuality," 331. *Bibliography*

Brainerd areas. (C-2, 4–6) In contrast, a gay man's published letter argued that homosexual persons should not be held to anti-promiscuity standards of heterosexuals. My response was that if homosexual persons wanted heterosexual support for equal rights from heterosexuals, his ethic would not be very effective. (C–3)

In 2001, an ELCA General Assembly resolution was passed that authorized denominational leadership to set up a church-wide dialogue after a committee of theologians and laity created a study guide outlining the two sides on the issue, including both theological and scientific stances. Congregational group discussions were encouraged and surveys were provided to be sent in, completed, and results compiled. A vote on greater acceptance was scheduled for 2007, but later changed to 2009. In that year, a resolution was passed accepting gays and lesbians, but the question of using the word "marriage" was left open.

At the time leading up to the vote, there were numerous letter–opinions in Minnesota newspapers from both ELCA members and non–members. Most of these letters criticized the process as much as the outcome. I responded to a number of these to correct serious misrepresentations. (C–4,5,6)

Several years after the ELCA decision there were increased letters about the moral and scientific aspects of homosexuality associated with state policy initiatives in Minnesota. One of these efforts was a push for a marriage amendment that would make marriage only between a man and a woman. However, this amendment failed to pass. In what appeared to be a backlash, within two years, Minnesota passed a law making same–sex marriage legal. Because many letters had misrepresentations of science, in some opinions I noted how this tactic undercut credibility of those opposed to homosexual equality. The change was helped by changes taking place in the business community, following the lead of the medical community. (C–1, 7)

Another type of misrepresentation in an opinion regarded homosexual parenting. In this case, some quoted study alleged that outcomes in "stable heterosexual households" selected by some criteria were compared to homosexual households without any selection criteria. Studies that used identical criteria showed no differences. (C–8)

A letter opposing attempted a "political correctness" (PC) argument starting with a premise that God was "so politically *incorrect*" when he "made them male and female" (italics added). This may have been some attempt at humor but without defining either PC or its "incorrect" meaning, it was difficult to make literal sense of the argument. Using a standard definition, it seemed to mean that when God made humans male and female, God was against efforts to counter injustices due to prejudice on sexuality issues. It was doubtful that was what the writer meant. (C–9)

Contraception and Abortion

In the sexuality controversies over contraception in the news, the fact that many women need contraceptive medications for other purposes is often overlooked. The two most common other indications are endometriosis and cystic ovary conditions. This need should not be ignored. (C–10,11)

It may seem odd that there were no opinions on abortion. This reflected the fact that there were very few opinions on the subject, other than some references to "millions of babies killed," usually related to attempts to downplay moral concerns about deaths from other causes in the news, such as gun deaths.

I strongly oppose abortion as a convenient alternative or correction to failed birth control. But at the same time it should be recognized that so-called "zero-tolerance" stances cross a different ethical line into other ethical breeches. For example, unsafe abortions increase maternal mortality. Such stances can breech respect for the autonomy of individual patients in their right to make decisions about their own health. And, as respected Catholic sister Joan Chittister has noted, there seems to be something defective in a morality that only wants a child born, but not policies that insure all children are adequately clothed, fed, and housed.

Summary

The modern scientific understanding of sexuality describes a relatively fixed variation in a spectrum of erotic attraction between poles of opposite–sex and same–sex attraction that is inherent and not subject to significant change. This reality is represented by the words heterosexual and homosexual, which were created in 1869, over 1500 years after the Bible was canonized. A small percentage of all variations are pathological (such as pedophilia), but all normal variations are benign such that they are able to live responsible moral livesn. Most emotional difficulties of persons with minority variations are caused by religious and societal hostility. There is no good evidence that the authors of biblical texts had any understanding of this spectrum. A paradigm shift in this understanding occurred in 1974 when the American Psychiatric Association declassified homosexuality as a disease and declared it a normal variant. This shifted the debate from the traditional moral depravity view of homosexuality to an issue of moral justice. One foundational biblical text for this justice cause is, "It is not good for the human being to be alone." (Genesis 2:18) Irrespective of how the ELCA outcome is viewed, my judgment is that the process was a model on how to conduct civil dialogue with fair representation of both sides on the issue.

D. Global Warming

With Bible in One Hand

Till It and Keep It

For biblical framing of the global warming issue, I often use three verses from the first three chapters of Genesis: "Till it and keep it." (Genesis 2:15) (D–1) I have found the books of two theologians especially helpful: *God and World in the Old Testament,* by Terrence Fretheim, emeritus professor of Old Testament at Luther Seminary,[7] and *Earth Honoring Faith,* by Larry Rasmussen, Reinhold Niebuhr Professor Emeritus of Social Ethics, Union Theological Seminary.[8]

The foundational verse for my proposition is, "And the Lord took the man and placed him in the Garden of Eden to till and to keep it." (Genesis 2:15) This action took place before the disobedience of Adam and Eve that according to the biblical account made childbirth and securing food sustenance come with "multiplied" pain, sweat and toil, generally interpreted to mean the introduction of sin into creation. (D–1) The important point here is that the tilling in a manner of "keeping" creation capable of optimum function was an ordained purposeful task unrelated to a coming moral disobedience. God gave those created in his own image a participative role in the creative and sustaining process. Furthermore, this opportunity or purposeful task was complicated but not lost because of sin: "The Lord God

---

7. Fretheim, *God and World in the Old Testament,* 50–54. Bibliography

8. Rasmussen, *Earth Honoring Faith,* 49. Bibliography

sent him forth from the Garden of Eden, to till the ground from which he was taken." (Genesis 3:23)

Self-centered human thinking has always complicated the task of tilling and keeping. One example is the effect two European philosophers had on the US founding fathers. Seemingly based mostly on interpretations of Genesis 1:26–28, Thomas Hobbes and John Locke used the "image of God" and "have dominion" phrases to justify assaults and exploitation of natural resources. (Genesis 1:26) Fretheim outlines how wrong this interpretation was because the original words of this text suggest instead a parenting or responsible steward relationship in which God gives over some of the creative function to humans to help bring order out of disorder. The soil was to be kept fruitful enough to grow plants whose roots, leaves, and fruits could nourish all terrestrial life.

In a conference that I attended, Professor Rasmussen suggested that what is needed instead of the traditional ways of thinking about the earth is a new way of life—a transformation. He quoted American philosopher William James regarding "ventures not seen, paths not trodden, to ends unknown." Science is important as a source of information, but people will not die for a pie chart of data. More is needed. Fear and terror move people, but so will hope. We could think of someone banging on a door, hoping someone is home. Rasmussen cited a story about a person who dreamed that he had been sent to another more barren planet and learned that its people talked about a much more beautiful planet somewhere called earth. He woke up seeing things differently.

The Bible's message is a potential source for necessary change. But there are obstacles. When asked about what message Rasmussen thought should be conveyed to those who deny the reality of global warming, he pointed out that whether or not skeptics believe global warming is real or not, if wrong, they or their descendants will have to live with the bad effects. It might therefore be prudent to start getting ready, and they might want to decide whether or not they want to be remembered in the category of former "flat earth" believers.

When asked about the effect of afterlife or "other world" religious belief, Rasmussen noted that as global world problems increase, the afterlife possibility seems more appealing, but it may, unfortunately cause increased negligence and lethargy about this world's problems. This is not a constructive effect of religion and can become grounds for skepticism directed at the value of biblical morality.

With Newspaper in One Hand

Global Warming Science

The usual graph of data used to display scientific evidence on global warming plots relevant facts on a vertical axis against time from 1750 to 2010 on a horizontal axis. Global average surface temperature slowly increased until about 1950, when temperatures started rising exponentially making a "hockey-stick" graph form. Other factors, including increasing atmospheric carbon dioxide levels, ozone layer depletion, and decrease in glacial ice, demonstrate similar patterns. In the same time frame, graphs of human consumption of dozens of manmade products showed remarkably similar patterns. These include paper products, fertilizer, real GDP, number of motor vehicles, and oil extraction from the earth. The correlations are tight. (D–1)

Major changes in a previously stable climate pattern happened about 1945 when the US went from a war economy with wage and price controls and rationing to a peacetime economy. But more than simply a natural change, there was a stimulus of consumption to increase tax revenue to help pay off the war debt, aided by the new advertising medium of television. For the last sixty-five years, this set the US on a course of being the world's top per capita producer of greenhouse gases, a spot it still holds, although China now exceeds the US in total production of harmful emissions.

The earth's changes in the 100 years are geophysical. Polar ice caps are decreasing, ocean temperatures are warming, jet streams are shifting, hurricanes and droughts are increasing. There are many warnings that we are far too many and too rich with "stuff," with the wrong kind of economies necessary to curb climate changes.

Basic science facts are that plant leaves and needles are nature's solar panels that transform the sun's energy into plant energy to fuel not only their own growth, but also the production of roots, seeds, and fruit that sustain other life. The unique chemical involved is chlorophyll, which transforms the sun's light into energy for plant growth. In the process, valuable oxygen is released necessary for human and animal respiration. A fundamental reality is that humans need chlorophyll more than chlorophyll needs humans. Humans have become the biggest threat to all life on the planet, and their own species is among the significantly vulnerable.

Lessons from Galileo

Because frequent opinions debunked global warming with airs of much certainty, I briefly reviewed the Galileo ecclesiastical trial on cosmology. Quotations from a surviving document demonstrate that the certainty of accusations against Galileo were similar to that of many global warming skeptics today. Galileo was judged to be wrong, but scientifically he turned out to be right. It was the Church that was wrong. (D–2) The outcome of the contemporary religion vs. science aspects of the global warming issue will likely be the same, and the credibility of Christianity will again likely suffer as a result. What is different from the Galileo affair is that the outcome then had little immediate actual scientific effect. The worst-case scenario related to global warming could be catastrophic.

A response from one global warming skeptic was surprising in that the writer did not directly address the global warming issue but instead claimed that Galileo was wrong. The author claimed that the sun in fact actually rotates around the earth. This response spurred other readers to weigh in, all supporting the view that Galileo was correct. The skeptic confirmed this was not a joke by doubling down. (D–3) Some observers thought this stance was likely derived from Creationist theology.

The notion that climate change is real and it has serious moral implications is supported by Pope Francis' "Laudat Si" encyclical. In it, he highlighted the scientific evidence and the bad implications of global warming, especially the predictions that its effects would hurt the poor of the world most and hurt them first. In 2015, the ELCA announced that "It joins with Pope Francis in asking world leaders to embrace our common responsibility as work continues on limiting climate change."

Summary

For decades, scientific evidence has been increasing that the earth is warming at unprecedented rates, and that human consumption is the major contributor. The greatest national contributor to this serious problem, both total and per capita, had been the US, until China passed the US in total emissions. For all of its supposedly advanced educational sophistication, the US populace seems to lead the world in climate skeptics. One letter called climate scientists liars, others argued against reality on the basis the benign nature of carbon dioxide, still others on the basis of God's covenant promise to Noah. Such ideologies make dialogue difficult. God gave human beings the capacity to increase knowledge of the natural world that can be used to improve life for all. But his knowledge can be selectively misused. The Bible has many texts that admonish good stewarding of this gift. One is the admonition to Adam, to, "Till the earth and keep it."

E. Gun Violence

With Bible in One Hand

The biblical basis I use for advocating stricter gun control is the total witness of Jesus' message and ministry. Such in–depth knowledge should especially be expected in a society that claims to be Christian. In representing the new Kingdom, Jesus boldly spoke truth to power in the name of justice, but he did this only by non-violent means. When Peter drew a knife to defend Jesus on the night of his arrest, Jesus rebuked him saying, "Put back your sword. Those who live by the sword will die by the sword." (Matthew 26:52) When Jesus sent the twelve out to proclaim the new kingdom they were instructed to "take nothing for their journey," which obviously included no knives, that would have been comparable to today's guns. (Mark 6:8) In a sinful world, governments need police departments to keep order, and armies and navies to defend the nation. But as much as can be reasonable, weapons should be limited to "well regulated" citizen possession to help keep them out of the hands of dangerous persons.

In some of my opinions on guns and war, I incorporated parts of theologian Douglas John Hall's relevant statements about the theology of the cross. This included: "God absorbed in his person the compulsion of the alien human spirit's desire to kill, and thereby create a new spirit within us" (see chapter 2). If the alien spirit of humankind is to kill, the biblical spirit for Christians should be to not kill (see page 17). And this translates into restricting access to weapons engineered for the primary purpose of killing or maiming living creatures. This should certainly include military grade weapons.

The pacifist non-violent Christian position regarding guns and war is most strict in the Mennonite and Quaker traditions, and they should be honored for this witness. We should also be reminded that Rev. Martin Luther King, Jr. was one of the best examples of a Christian boldly protesting and speaking truth to power regarding justice on the basis of biblical theology.

With Newspaper in One Hand.

Guns as a Public Health Problem

Next to the Bible, my ethical world has been framed by my professional ethical tradition. Therefore, it is natural to refer to the position-statement on guns published by the American College of Physicians (ACP)[9] The ACP is the professional association for internal medicine specialists in the U.S.

Some of relevant statistics published in the ACP position paper are: "firearms in the home pose more of a threat to members of the household than to intruders . . . the risk of suicide is fivefold greater . . . the risk of homicide three times . . . the greatest from family members and close acquaintances . . . More teenagers die of gunshot wounds than of all natural causes combined, for every death involving firearms, twice as many need hospitalization and five times as many need outpatient care . . . the financial costs can be staggering . . . up to $15 billion annually in total direct and indirect medical costs, including temporary or permanent loss of work."[10]

Not all of the recommendations of the ACP will be reviewed here, but they include banning military style assault rifles, banning high–capacity magazines, tight background checks, and closing gun-show and other loopholes. More recently the ACP, along with five other medical groups plus the American Bar Association made a similar position statements calling for stricter gun control.

The ACP stance was melded with my gun background experience in formulating my opinion stance on gun control. My father taught me how to use shotguns in rural Minnesota in a county where both pheasants and migrating ducks used to be in abundance. I taught my sons how to use shotguns. I was in the U.S Army Medical Corps at the height of the Viet Nam war. In basic training I learned how to shoot a predecessor to the modern assault rifle. I saw some of the body and psychic damage of many wounded in that war. Twenty-five years later I was selected as a juror on a gun store robbery-murder trial related to a rural Minnesota gun-running operation. These experiences all affected my moral view on guns.

9. *Annals of Internal Medicine*, 1998. 236–41. *Bibliography*
10. *Annals of Internal Medicine*, 2015, 311–13. *Bibliography*

The NRA response to this public health reality and the medical recommendations on how to deal with it is that more guns in private hands
will result in fewer per capita deaths, with the less regulation, the better. The
question, therefore is, since the US has six times more than the average per
capita ownership of the other nineteen top industrialized democracies in
the world, why does the US have 2.5 times the average per capita deaths of
those countries? The relationship is supposed to be the opposite.

Guns. Newtown, School Prayer, and the Bible

Guns and the biblical faith issues occasionally appear in the news linked
together, more often than not with attempts to make them seem compatible
rather than incompatible. After a child was killed by a gun, an editorial in
the Minneapolis *Star Tribune* was published on the incident *along* with a
pastor's guest opinion. I responded to both with an essay that began:

> The irony of the coincidence on the editorial page Nov 29 should
> not go unnoticed. The editorial poignantly described one of thou-
> sands of domestic hand-gun-caused tragedies, and an opinion by a
> local pastor blames lack of prayer in the public schools for violence
> in homes (along with a host of other problems). The connection
> is more than coincidental. Those invoking the Constitution as the
> basis for public school prayer more often than not use the same
> claim against gun control.

I suggested a political compromise: allow a prayer in schools every
morning that asks God to prevent any shooting in return for tightening gun
control. (E–2) The NRA, of course, would never agree to that. I noted my
military and robbery-murder jury experiences and concluded with: "I believe less faith in guns and more demonstrable faith that would limit guns
would represent more authentic faith and be better than arming ourselves,
while forcing our prayers on others." Another letter made a similar claim in
asserting that much of the US gun violence was because God was left out
of our schools. (E–5)

Shortly after the Newtown, Connecticut elementary school shooting,
a syndicated guest opinion titled, "Why was God AWOL at Newtown?" was
published in the *Brainerd Dispatch*. (E–3) This opinion was an example of
an attempt to construct a moral framework from which to judge the use of
military weaponry in the Newtown grade school. Its foundational stance
was, "Bad things happen. It's an inescapable reality of life." The journalist

then went on to quote from Reinhold Niebuhr's Serenity Prayer, plus other references on Niebuhr's view of the role of anxiety in human behavior. My response outlined how theologian Marjorie Suchockie built on Niebuhr's anxiety thesis in relationship to her interest in human violence. In one of her books, *The Fall to Violence*, after citing a tragic gun-death of a young girl, she commented:

> Someone made the guns available to the children . . . Corporate greed for ever greater profits from gun sales results in an incredible proliferation of guns throughout American culture, all under the reasoning that if everyone has guns, everyone can protect the self from everyone else, and so honor the sacred "right to bear arms" guaranteed to every American. Do not those who traffic in developing the taste for violence share in the guilt? . . . The American obsession with guns and violence . . . is our attempt to delude ourselves into believing that we can confine our violence through channeling it into an arena or ring, and that we can turn the power of our televisions off, and so control the violence that we safely allow into our lives. But anxiety mocks our control. Violence, not death, is at the root of our anxieties, and our attempts to channel violence simply increases its ceaseless flow.[11]

Two reader opinions made similar claims that unfettered gun freedom did not compromise faith in God, and a third letter eleven days later praised these letters, adding some reasons on why guns and faith do not constitute a problem. (E–7) These bold statements might be expected to be accompanied by some supportive biblical text references. They were not, and instead one argument was that because the words gun and violence are not synonyms, there could therefore be no logical relationship between these two words. My response to this reasoning used the definition of violence as "a swift, injurious force," which is what guns deliver, making the relationship of guns to violence a tight one.

One of the letters claiming guns did not compromise biblical faith went further to claim that decreased societal faith in God led to increased gun violence. There was no reason given why this connection couldn't work in reverse, so I argued that increased personal reliance on guns may be acts of faith in guns that displaces authentic faith in God. I also noted that if this decrease in societal faith linked to levels of gun violence in the US were

---

11. Suchockie, *The Fall to Violence*, 139. *Bibliography*

true, the US must comparatively be one of the most godless of the twenty most developed nations in the world. (E–5)

One syndicated columnist opinion was titled, "God and Human Nature." The author never defined human nature as used in the essay, and the references were only to the negative traits of the mentally ill and criminals, as if this were the major problem. This fit with a reasoning that stricter gun laws will do no good. Other human traits were never referred to, such as those cited by poet William Blake, including, "mercy, pity, peace and love." Consideration of the whole spectrum of human traits can raise the question of whether or not there is a difference in the proportions of these different human traits in gun owner-enthusiasts and persons who see no need to own guns. Or, is there something about guns that can change human nature toward the worse? (E–4)

Political Reach of the NRA

The political reach of the NRA was the subject of one of my opinions after the NRA's ability to block the approval of Dr. Vikel Murthy for Surgeon General of the United States, especially when this action caused the U.S. to be without anyone in this position when the Ebola epidemic broke out. This political move was made because Dr. Murthy had once stated that gun violence should be considered a public health issue. He was, of course, simply stating the position of the ACP noted earlier, and also that of many other specialty groups. This was even after Dr. Murthy had promised not to do anything about gun control if approved as Surgeon General. It isn't bad enough that guns are a health issue, the NRA wants to also adversely affect other health issues to show how it can flex its political might. (E–8)

The Bell Tolls Again

After the Parkland, FL school shooting, a published letter I wrote ended with this partial quotation from John Donne's poem: "No man is an island, entire of itself; every man is a piece of the continent, a part of the main . . . Any man's death diminishes me, because I am involved in mankind. And therefore, never send to know for whom the bell tolls; it tolls for thee." (E–14)

Summary

The scientific aspect of my stance on gun violence has been based primarily on the position papers first published decades ago by the American College of Physicians, the specialty association in which I had been a member. Most other specialty organizations have similar statements. Some basic facts are that the direct cost of medical treatment for gun injuries is about $4 billion per year and the additional indirect costs are upwards of $15 billion annually. The U.S. has the highest per capita private ownership of guns in the world and is near the top of advanced democracies in per capita suicides and homicides. The basic problem is the easy availability of guns, thanks to the NRA, along with their ideology that we should focus only on human factors to reduce violence. Jesus, of course, told Peter, "Put back your sword." The core biblical stance since Jesus has been to exhaust every possible non–violent means before resorting to violence (page 17). Strict gun controls are biblically more ethical than relatively unrestricted access to guns. Attempts at rational combinations of gun rights with biblical faith are common in the press, but usually do not easily pass rational or ethical tests.

F. War, Torture, and Terrorism

With Bible in One Hand

War

A Christian stance on war obviously depends on the nature of the threat involved. But in any case, a good text to start with in formulating a Christian stance on war could be Jesus' response to Pilate when he was asked, "Are you king of the Jews?" Jesus' response was, "My kingdom is not of this world. If it were, my disciples would have fought to prevent my arrest." (John 18:36) Many people of Jesus' time expected the Messiah to be a warrior like David to lead their people to independence. To them, Jesus was a disappointment. Pilate, however, was put at ease by Jesus' answer to this question about kingship. Powerful rulers want religious leaders to keep their members other–world focused so that political leaders can make the worldly power decisions uninhibited by moral activists. One can argue that the above statement of Jesus means the Church should stay out of government affairs. Or, one can argue that the other-world "security message" in the theology of the cross should embolden believers to speak truth to power, insisting war should be a last resort. That's what Bonhoeffer and Barth did.

A book titled *Pro-Life / Pro-Peace* by former ELCA Lutheran bishop, Lowell Erdahl, began with the statement: "Many of my pro-life friends don't like my views on war and capital punishment, and many pro-peace friends don't like my stands on abortion and mercy killing."[12]

Thus there is a mixed meaning of the word "Pro-life" in American Christianity. In reflecting on why this might be, Bishop Erdahl noted that, "We glory in the heroes of the American Revolution and never doubt that they were justified in killing the British, who were about as accommodating as any 'oppressor' could be. We think of defensive wars against unjustified aggressors as justified, but was it equally justified to kill British soldiers for this kind of "liberation?"[13]

A favorite American war song proclaims that, "As he died to make men holy, let us die (or live) to make men free." Bishop Erdahl noted that the famous preacher Harry Emerson Fosdick commented that what we really should sing is, "let us kill to make men free"—Jesus sacrificed himself rather than to use violence.[14] He did not sacrifice himself using violence. "Die" in a Christian context usually indicates a willingness to be an unarmed martyr for faith and justice, not marching off in crusades, preemptive wars, or promoting guns.

Bishop Erdahl's book has a fifty-page chapter on a biblical perspective for war, including emphasis on the horrible nature of any future war that involves use of nuclear weapons. War decisions are made in government rooms of power. The question for every Christian is what constitutes the most biblical stance for the Christian citizen. Theologian Marcus Borg summarizes a two-part Christian political stance that could apply to war: "I have learned that much of the Bible is political in the sense of being a radical critique of such (worldly) systems, and an advocacy of another way of pursuing our common life together, all in the name of God."[15] This was a part of Moses' confrontation with the pharaoh in Egypt, the prophets' protest against the power and wealth of the monarchies in Israel (pages 25–28), and New Testament Christianity's stance in the context of the Roman

12. Erdahl, *Pro-Life / Pro-Peace*, 11. *Bibliography*

13. Ibid., 22.

14 Fosdick, "Putting Christ into Uniform."

15. Borg, *Convictions*, 148. *Bibliography*

Empire. A constant critical eye is necessary because of the nature of power in the hands of humans.

Torture

A biblical theological stance regarding torture may be framed by the same texts used for gun violence and war. In addition, we could be reminded that it is oversimplified to state that Jesus died for the sake of humankind. Jesus didn't die from an accident or an assassin's knife. That he died after being tortured and crucified has meaning beyond a special way of showing the magnitude of God's love through Jesus' suffering. His innocent suffering came at the hands of human beings. Most biblical theologies claim Jesus was a revelation of the nature of God. In Luther's theology of the cross this means a revelation of the suffering nature of God, and his special concern for those who suffer—especially unjustly. Thus, Jesus accepted torture not to sanction his followers' use of torture, but the opposite. Disciples should have a "new spirit" that refuses to engage in torture and instead practice the New Testament spirit of what is right, which is to "suffer for righteousness sake." (Matthew 5:10) Independent of all this, but consistent with it, medical ethics manuals state that physician participation in torture is always immoral.

The book of Acts records a history of the start of the church. In chapter 5, after Peter and some Christians were imprisoned and released for their preaching and healing, "they left the council, rejoicing that they were counted worthy to suffer dishonor for the name." (Acts 5:41) In its first 300 years, the early church was a persecuted minority and there is no evidence that they ever resorted to violence, either individually or collectively. They were ready to suffer torture and death "for Jesus sake." In modern Christianity, this history seems forgotten.

Terrorism

Looking for biblical texts or theological themes of relevance for formulating a Christian ethical posture on terrorism is not simple. It is difficult to argue against a government taking some measures of self-defense in the face of terrorism. But Christians should be on guard against an ideology in which the brutal nature of terrorism blinds ability to perceive how the US may have spawned terrorism against itself. It is easy for a type of patriotism to create a false feeling of moral superiority that exempts the US from ethical norms in dealing with the issue. In the view of many observers, 9/11 should be viewed as a response of some in the Muslim world what they perceived as deliberate attempts to humiliate certain Muslim groups over the previous seventy years. It was not primarily over a conflicting religion or ideology.

In this context, two biblical themes may stand out more than others. The first relates to being as honest as possible with ourselves. Under the spotlight of root causes, part of a quotation from Douglas John Hall bears repeating: "It can in fact be argued (and is) that the current [2003] bellicosity of the militant forms of Islam represents a reaction of the Muslim world to its humiliation by the powerful technocratic West . . . which just happens to be the most avowedly Christian of all the nations of the world."[16] (see pages 18–19). The facts contributing to this humiliation will not be reviewed here, but they are substantial. A sense of humiliation is likely what caused Bin Laden to engineer 9/11, which then led to a preemptive US led invasion of Iraq on false justification, which probably was the main cause of ISIS formation.

The second relevant biblical theme that should be kept in mind is the record of the Hebrew prophets' warning of God's judgment to Israel and Judah for falling away from their covenant after rising to prosperity in the promised land. Following this, God used comparatively ungodly nations to work justice in history. Historians may see human forces behind events in which the biblical view sees God's invisible finger of justice at work. God is not immune to using "ungodly" nations to bring justice against others that claim to be the godliest. It might also be appropriate to remember the biblical dictum that, "To whom much is given, much is expected. (Luke12:48)

With Newspaper in One Hand

War

A reader opinion alleged that *failure* of an avowed Christian nation to go to war in retribution for killing of some American Christians constituted *fulfillment* of Jesus' prophecy that believers would "be hated for his names sake." (F–1) A similar guest opinion proposed that American Christians should join the battle with our mighty armed national brotherhoods in

16. Hall, *The Cross in our Context*, 4. Bibliography

"wielding a sword of protection for world-wide persecuted Christians." Its author claimed that Christians have a duty to defend that kingdom of God because "Christian men formed police departments and national armies and navies." (F–2)

In the perspective of Jesus' life and teachings, such claims seem unbiblical. First, as already noted, Christians in the early church never lifted a sword against Rome, and yet they grew in numbers rapidly. The Church and the Kingdom of God are not to be spread by means of killing because unless obviously defensive it seriously corrupts the biblical theology of the cross into a perverse theology of glory (see pages 19–20). Second, foreign persons have many reasons to dislike Americans without linking it to a "for Jesus sake" text. A more likely reason why many Muslims dislike the US is the hypocrisy of such melding God and guns "for Jesus sake."

Jesus was hated by many because he spoke truth by non–violent means that exposed moral hypocrisy. Jesus was also hated by many because he spoke truth to power about injustices of his time, He threatened the collusion of religious leaders with the Roman government. Martin Luther King, Jr. remains the premier model of non-violent activism for justice.

Another opinion was less explicit about the national use of violent means but did not rule it out. Its general theme was that the US should "Stop the Madness" caused by Muslims. (F–3) This opinion also linked the prominence of the word "submission" in Islamic writing and linked it to an alleged Islamic purpose to militarily make the entire world come under political submission to Islamic rule. The opinion author made no reference to the "submission to God" literal meaning of the word *Islam*, and by this insulted all Muslims. Added to this danger was the fact that none of the letters distinguished radical terrorists from the rest of the peace-loving Muslims, both in the US and the world. All three letters shared the ingredients of documents potentially useful as jihadist terrorist propaganda tools.

A letter–opinion suggested Democrats need to get "back to the Bible" more than Republicans do, and asked rhetorically, "What do you think?" The writer gave no examples, so I chose the new administration's drastic cutting of the State Department while pushing hard for marked increases in military spending (while the U.S. military is larger than the next six nations combined). Since the Bible uses the "soft power" of the word and not coercive "hard power" of firepower, I suggested the conservative foreign policy trend was in the wrong direction, and probably not to God's liking. (A–13)

Torture

"We need to return to God and Patriotism" was the main theme an opinion letter that I chose to take some exception to. (F–4) My view had long been that attempts to mix God and patriotism, like mixing God and personal gun rights, must be done very carefully—if at all. The opinion was not explicit in stating what we should return to. Therefore, in an attempt to show that there is no agreement on how patriotic acts are best defined, I used some pro and con views of torture to illustrate that persons on both sides of the torture question could consider themselves patriotic. If one has one ethic for Christians and another for patriotism, this becomes a rationalized "two-sphere" ethic that Dietrich Bonhoeffer rejected in favor of a "one sphere" holistic biblical ethic (see pages 34–36).

This opinion of mine brought a very critical response from a third person, suggesting that my stance was simplistic or naive. But that response never refuted my basic thesis that different persons that both regard themselves as patriotic can have different views on policies. (F–5) The only substantive claim that this critic made on the issue of torture was that waterboarding was directly responsible for the demise of Osama bin Laden. My response to this assertion was to quote Leon Panetta's statement that the only thing learned from torture was that Bin Laden had a currier, and that was already known from other sources and means.

There are other realities that I never introduced into in this exchange but would have had I chosen to continue the dialogue. One is that medical ethics manuals such as that of the *American College of Physicians* state, "Physician participation in torture is never morally defensible."[17] The Bush administration retained two psychologists for eight million dollars to oversee water boarding at Guantanamo prison. This caused them to breech their ethical code. The amount of money paid for this waterboarding says something about the ethics of that policy.

Everyone with any biblical knowledge knows how Jesus was put to death. Torture and crucifixion were not rare or unique in Jesus' world. The Romans put many thousands to death by crucifixion. Despite this, most Christians suspect how Jesus was put to death has special significance. Just because scourging and using a crown of thorns are not used today does not justify other immoral means of dubious value.

17. Snyder, ACP *Ethics Manual*, 2. *Bibliography*

Terrorism

I wrote three opinion responses on terrorism. One of these opinions was in response to contrasting syndicated opinions by conservative journalists Charles Krauthammer, and David Brooks. These were just after the Paris nightclub massacre in response to the Charlie Hebdo sarcastic depictions of Islam. Krauthammer somewhat defended the publication using sarcasm, while David Brooks' column was titled, "I am not Charlie Hebdo." (F–6) Sarcastic denigrations of other people can turn deadly. Insulting others is not a biblical virtue.

Jihadists may contrast themselves from Krauthammer's view by quoting the Koran: "Defend yourself against your enemies, but do not attack first. God hates the aggressor" (Koran 2:190).[18] The US will always be accused by many as the aggressor in the Iraq invasion. It is easy for jihadists to point to that event as demonstrating how the US is the immoral aggressor. In so doing they think we gave up the moral high ground.

Another editorial was about two related serious issues faced by the US: polarized political division and jihadist terrorists. I agreed with opinions identifying these issues as serious, but I was critical of some opinion exchanges because I did not think they offered positive suggestions. Everyone wants jihadist terrorists identified and denied rights. But many of these same citizens do not want to be inconvenienced by laws that restrict weaponry that is easily available to potential terrorists. (F–7)

Summary

War, meaning "a major armed conflict between nations," signifies failure to keep peace. It also represents a moral failure of humankind. From the life, death, and teachings of Jesus, Christians should stand for doing everything possible to prevent war short of falling victim to an evil dictatorial power. Some defensive wars may be inevitable. Christians should insist that their governments strictly adhere to just war principles. Unfortunately, the Christian Church historically has too often taken unjustified positions on going into armed conflict, a perversion of cross theology into glory theology. An important function of government State Departments is to prevent wars. State departments should match defense departments in government importance. Nuclear restriction treaties are more biblical than war.

18. *The Koran*, 29, (2:89). *Bibliography*

Predilection to torture and terrorism come with war and neither are biblically justified. Excessive patriotic militarism or insulting indecency undercuts positive biblical influence leading to a decrease in cultural morality and increased violence.

G. Refugees

With Bible in One Hand

A dictionary definition of refugee is, "A person who flees for refuge or safety, especially to a foreign country, as in a time of war." The issues related to refugees overlap to some extent with those of immigrants. The question of whether or not the Bible has any texts relevant to refugees should start with consideration of three relevant facts. First, according to biblical history, the Israelites were once refugees from slavery in Egypt, and God took care of them during their years in the wilderness. Second, during the years of creating and maintaining their new society in Palestine, there always seemed to be non-Israelites in their midst, for whom they were expected to care. Third, Joseph, Mary, and Jesus took refuge from Herod in Egypt. (Matthew 2:13–15) Some Old Testament references are:

> You shall not oppress a stranger or oppress him; for you were strangers in the land of Egypt.
>
> Exodus 23:9.

> Thus, says the Lord, if you truly execute justice with one another, if you do not oppress the alien, the fatherless or the widow. . .then I will let you dwell in this place. . .
>
> Jeremiah 7:6.

> Thus, says the Lord. . .do no wrong or violence to the alien, the fatherless, and the widow, nor shed innocent blood in this place.
>
> Jeremiah 22:3

> Behold you princes of Israel. . .the sojourner suffers extortion in your midst, the fatherless and the widow are wronged in you.
>
> Ezekiel 22:6

> Then I will draw near to you for judgment . . . I will be a witness against the adulterers. . . against those who thrust aside the sojourner, and do not fear me, says the Lord of hosts.
>
> Malachi 3:5

Jesus' obvious preferential concern for "the lost, the least and the little" supports a view that Christians should cultivate this attitude in gratitude for his sacrifice to free people of faith from the bondage of sin and its consequences. Jesus' parable of the Good Samaritan is relevant. (Luke 10:37) Jesus responded to the question, "When did we see thee and welcome thee?" with the answer, "Even as you did it unto one of the least of these my brethren, you did it unto me." (Mathew 25:45)

Near the end of the letter to the Hebrews, the author writes, "Let brotherly love continue. Do not neglect to show hospitality to strangers, for thereby many have entertained angels unawares." (Hebrews 13:1)

In some nations, patriotism and fear (anxiety) are mixed, often with links to religion. Such mixing degrades both the religion and its potential positive effects on behalf of refugees. Thus, although individually many Americans might help by contributing money to relief agencies like Lutheran World Relief, Catholic Charities, and the Red Cross, when it comes to national policies to help refugees resulting from wars that the US initiated, there is considerable anti-refugee sentiment. Moral considerations would say this risk should be diligently guarded against, but it usually isn't (see also pages 27–29). The refugee issue has been linked with Muslims in the American mind and policy because most of the world's refugees seeking asylum in the twenty–first century are linked to 9/11 and its subsequent wars.

With Newspaper in One Hand

Moral Man and Immoral Society

As already noted, Reinhold Niebuhr was one of the most prominent American theologians in US history He laid a foundation for Christian ethics applied to groups in his book, *Moral Man and Immoral Society*.[19] Niebuhr observed that humans have great individual capacity to act with compassion for the well–being of others. However, when they organize

---

19. Niebuhr, *Moral Man and Immoral Society*, 6–16. *Bibliography*

into likeminded competitive groups, the group ego morality takes on a hypocrisy and selfishness not characteristic of its individual members. The phenomenon is roughly proportional to the power relationships involved, so risk to the well–being of people is most pronounced in nation-states.

At a time when the Syrian refugee crisis was getting more and more attention in the news, a series of anti-Muslim reader opinions made no distinction between the relatively few jihadist radicals and most other Muslims, essentially painting all Muslims as terrorists. The presidential primary campaign debates were occurring at that time and one candidate likened Muslims to dogs, some rabid. Others said only Christian Arabs should be accepted as refugees. There should be special IDs, watch lists, and Mosque surveillance. We should carpet–bomb the Caliphate into oblivion. Similar to what was noted in the previous section on terrorism, these candidate-statements and letters could be used as terrorist recruitment tools.

If one applies the above Niebuhr thesis to the Iraq war, it can be argued that the ethical justification of the Iraq invasion was an expedient secular ends-justifies-the-means ethic in a fear and power-toxic context. This clouded moral judgment and compromised the outcome. A more prudent Christian ethic such as Niebuhr's might have avoided the whole war. The same moral risk of bad outcomes could apply to the refugee question. (G–1)

Christian Compassion and Muslim Bans

One opinion alleged that the US was the most generous and compassionate nation in the world, and this fact should justify not admitting refugees but instead use money to show distant compassion. The US is high on the list in terms of dollars given for refugees, but not that high in terms of average per capita money given. (G–4)

A May 2017 opinion alleged that a judge's ruling on challenges to President Trump's travel bans showed bias in blocking refugees. (G–5) The letter did not acknowledge the President's campaign statement that he would order "a total and complete shutdown on all Muslims entering the country until we can find out what the h*** is going on." This ban was to be for 90 days for most countries, but the opinion letter was written long after that 90-day period had passed, and there had been no terrorist attacks in that time period. This statement showed that regards both intent of the ban and the stated time it was to cover, the judge's ruling was reasonable (G–5).

Child Refugee Crisis at the Border

In the summer of 2014 a different refugee crisis occurred at the Texas-Mexico border with a surge of refugee children seeking asylum from the violence of the Central American countries they were fleeing. A guest opinion by a syndicated columnist blamed President Obama's views on immigration for the problem and suggested that we should instead abide by the Constitution. (G–2)

The author neglected to mention, however, that President G.W. Bush and Congress passed two laws on how children should be uniquely processed, consistent with Bush's "compassionate conservatism" agenda. Border agents were following these laws, meaning the Constitution thereby was being honored. The columnist also ignored the fact that part of the root cause of the crises was decades of huge US illicit drug purchases coming across the border and the related gun-gang culture the US exported to South and Central America. The crisis may have been part of a bill come due.

Some stories in the news from the US southern border and inside countries like Honduras are chilling. Many mothers sent daughters because gangs were threatening to force young girls into nonconsensual sex. One who resisted was raped and killed and then her body parts were distributed along streets to schools as warning to others. Young boys are threatened with gun death if they didn't join gangs. Those who line up with strong anti-refugee sentiment want to quickly turn these children back to the terror of a life of fear and suffering without even a hearing.

Zero Tolerance Refugee Policy

The zero tolerance refugee and asylum policy that the Trump administration implemented in April, 2018 made the 2014 crisis pale by comparison. It is reviewed in the Postscript Trumpism section (pages 137–139).

Summary

From the advice of the Old Testament prophets to give aid to sojourners to Jesus' parable of the Good Samaritan, the biblical admonition is clearly that gratitude to God should be expressed by helping the unfortunate, and not only those of one's own race or nationality. Abraham's family escaped famine in Palestine by becoming refugees in Egypt, and generations later when they had become slaves, God made them refugees and gave them a new land, which they were to never forget. Mary, Joseph and the baby Jesus had to become temporary refugees in Egypt to escape Herod's threats. US policy has usually attempted to reflect this refuge principle. But recent Trump policy changes have clearly turned in the opposite direction. A promise to DACA immigrants was broken, and sobbing children have been taken away from parents at the border, many poorly unaccounted for, and many of whom may never be reunited with their families. This has become a new face of "family values" in the US.

H. Politics

With Bible in One Hand

In formulating a biblical framework from which to critique political events and recent government actions in the news, there are many of the same ambiguities that there are in relating the Bible to terrorism: "Render unto Caesar. . ., My kingdom is not of this world," etc. Jesus proclaimed no new programs to reform society, nor did he outline any new designs for morally ideal governments. However, like Nathan and the other biblical prophets, Jesus spoke truth to power about practices that flouted God's righteous order. Pilate was told, "You would have no power over me unless it were delivered to you from above." (John 19:11) An often repeated theme of Jesus was the summation of the law: "Love your neighbor as yourself." (Mark 12:31)

Similar to money and possessions, governing power is a temporary possession to be handled like a steward given responsibility by another to use it wisely. There will be an accounting. Jesus also exposed the hypocrisy in how many of his day acted with regard to the laws or rules they were living under at the time, both Jewish and Roman. One could use these facts to argue both that religion should serve as a watchdog moral critic or that the Church should stay out of political affairs.

A politically relevant text of Paul is the thirteenth chapter of Romans that begins with: "Let every person be subject to the governing authorities. But in the context of the entire Bible, this admonition is not unconditional. Miriam disobeyed Pharaoh when she hid the baby Moses. Mary and Joseph disobeyed Herod when they fled with Jesus to Egypt. (Matthew 2:14–15)

Paul argued, "We must obey God rather than men. (Acts 2:25) Dietrich Bonhoeffer wrote, "the Christian's duty of obedience is binding on him until the government directly compels him to offend against the divine commandment"[20] (see page 137).

Bonhoeffer's views from this work cannot be easily simplified. But it may be worth noting that in one section Bonhoeffer outlined four ethical mandates for Christians. These mandates are labor (vocation), marriage, government, and the church in the world: "God has imposed all four on all men. This means that there can be no retreating from a 'secular' into a 'spiritual' sphere. There can be only the practice, the learning, of the Christian life under these four mandates of God."[21] One of government's primary functions is to preserve all four mandates, because all four are legitimated by God. Every master is under a higher master who has been deputized. One of the responsibilities of the church is to remind the world of this.

A reasonable conclusion is that if Christians anywhere want to be an influence in preventing what happened in Germany leading to World War-II, they should find ethical ways to have a positive moral influence on their government. But to accomplish this they must first be able to have civil dialogue with one another over partisan differences in framing issues with the Bible.

With Newspaper in One Hand

Justice

The eleven opinions in the politics category may be divided into five subcategories: justice, criticisms of President Obama, partisan criticisms of others, Trumpism, and partisan incivility.

The general definition of justice I used to frame my opinions issues is the moral principle of determining right conduct (or righteousness), leading to administration of deserved punishment or reward. In other words, justice is about trying to curb unrighteous behavior. Unrighteous behavior is a direct offense to God because righteousness is one of the primary spiritual realities of God as revealed in the Bible, compassion being the other primary attribute. For millennia, controversies in organized societies over just vs. unjust actions have usually been resolved under a judge in public

20. Bonhoeffer, *Ethics*, 332–353. *Bibliography*
21. Ibid., 207–208.

hearings, with or without juries. Concerns about whether public policies and jury decisions properly conform to justice standards are parts of ongoing controversies, often evident in newspaper editorial pages. (H–3)

An abstract question of how justice priorities and principles might be different in opposing candidates or officeholders was the subject of a reader opinion. No specific persons were cited so I raised the question using examples of both former Minnesota governor Tim Pawlenty and former US Representative Michelle Bachman. Both openly identified themselves as Christians. This example was not to suggest that they were unjust, but to ask if it is it fair to compare how any specific stance of avowed Christian candidates match with biblical precepts. Another question is whether or not Christian candidates should be regarded as more trustworthy than someone without such an affirmation. (H–2) There are many reasons to doubt that they are.

Criticisms of President Obama

President Obama was subjected to many criticisms not only in public media but also via the internet, some in so–called political emails or urban legends for purposes of forwarding and not publication. These are easy for an editor to miss. One such letter falsely alleged excessive executive orders compared to previous presidents. (H–5)

Another letter accused President Obama of a lie based on a casual 2006 statement, "We deserve better" in reference to the economy at the time. This statement was made over two years before Obama became President, and this was compared only to the writer's subjective judgment that after two years in office the economy did not match the writer's again subjective judgment of "better." But Obama's statement was not a promise to meet any standard, so the allegation filled no criteria of a lie. (H–6)

Constructive vs. Negative Criticism

A state representative's appearance at a school award ceremony prompted a series of partisan letters. All letters were respectful except for one, which accused another letter's author commenting on the event of using an ad hominem attack, a straw man argument, and multiple falsehoods After reviewing the letter in question, I responded with definitions of each of these different allegations followed by my judgment that nothing in the letter fit any of my definitions I therefore concluded that the critic's letter fit definitions of what the critic accused the other reader of. (J–9) This brought a rare harsh response, but despite this, the critic of my opinion did not rebut my specific judgments. Such occasions were rare, with most exchanges vibrant and good-natured.

To address the topic of public civility with factual honesty, I wrote an opinion on what I viewed as a good example of "positive partisanship" between two of our founding fathers, Thomas Jefferson and Alexander Hamilton. (H–1) This opinion on Jefferson-Hamilton was based largely on the book, *Thomas Jefferson* by Jon Meachem, which I had recently read.[22] A main theme of the book was about how these two men, while almost polar opposites in their philosophies of democratic governance, dealt with each other with respect and civility. I suggested that we would do well to look to the political practices of Washington, Jefferson, and Hamilton to get ourselves out of the partisan gridlock we are so often in.

If these two men could, they would likely admonish us that partisanship is a permanent reality. We should accept this fact, get on with it and work together, or we may seriously harm the Republic. This perspective is a good note on which to end this section on politics.

Summary

Jesus told Pilate, "You would have no power over me unless it were delivered to you from above." (John 19:11) Like money, governing power is a temporary possession to be handled like a steward given responsibility by another to use wisely (see pages 33–34). According to the Bible, there will likely be an accounting for all human relationships. But especially in democracies, both politicians and citizens should have a steward responsibility for their right to vote and communicating among one another with truthfulness and civility. Some published opinions misrepresented the number and content of President Obama's executive orders, his Attorney General's comments on a major issue, and one opinion writer misrepresented another with allegations of using logical fallacies and falsehoods when nothing fit any such criteria. These actions reflect a negative and un–Christian polarity that diminishes governing effectiveness. This should be considered serious business because a major function of government is to execute justice, something that is difficult to do. All citizens could learn some lessons about

22. Meacham, *Thomas Jefferson: The Art of Power. Bibliography*

how to hold different views with civility from the relationship of founders like Thomas Jefferson and Alexander Hamilton.

I. Economics

With Bible in One Hand

Unlike the previous section on politics and government, where relevant biblical texts may seem more implicit than explicit, there is no difficulty in finding Old or New Testament texts relevant to money and economics as it relates to the economic well-being of any society. It is worth another reminder that the history of Abraham's descendants as a nation started with the Exodus out of slavery in Egypt. The "promised land" was to be where God's "chosen" would have much greater economic freedom from economic hardship. God's commandments were "For your good," and if followed there need be "no poor among you." (Deuteronomy. 10:13, 15:4)

About ten percent of the recorded words of Jesus in the gospels are about money and possessions. In addition, many of his words relate to the broader theme of living as God's stewards of what we have title to rather than owners who can simply do as they wish with material possessions. Individual stewardship should be matched by societal and governmental steward responsibilities.

A main theme of the Bible is the warning that moral failure risks negative consequences. How this relates to the mixture of earnest effort vs. deliberate disobedience, and God's grace vs. judgment in terms of temporal vs. eternal consequences cannot be easily defined. But it seems fair to state that no possibilities can be guaranteed to be off the table. To claim eternal certainty while flouting admonitions regarding economic or any other area of stewardship seems risky. Salvation is by faith, but evidence of faith comes from morally responsible living, which good governance facilitates— "You will know them by their fruits." (Matthew 7:16, 20)

In many times and ways Jesus taught that wealth disparity is not consistent with what the Kingdom of God stands for: "Blessed are you poor ... Woe to you who are rich ... " "It is harder for a rich man to enter the kingdom than ... " The rich fool built a bigger barn to store more grain than he needed; After meeting Jesus, Zacchaeus the tax collector gave half his possessions to the poor and paid back anyone he cheated four times over; "Where your treasure is, there your heart will me also;" "You cannot serve God and possessions;" "Even as you did it to the least of these my brethren, you did it unto me."

Jesus' parable about the rich man and Lazarus may have special poignancy for the US government's Constitutional role to economically "provide for the general welfare." (Luke 16:19–31) The rich man wore fine clothing and dined sumptuously. Lazarus was a destitute poor man with sores the dogs licked, lying at the gate of the rich man who gave him only crumbs from his table to eat. The two men may be seen as representing the two extremes of a tiered domination economic system legitimated by a dubious religious view that riches are evidence of the blessings of being good no matter how ill–gotten the riches are. Jesus' parable reverses good vs. bad labels of laziness that allege the cause of being poor is usually the poor person's indolence.

With Newspaper in One Hand

Biblical and Non-biblical Economics

Pope Francis' 2013 apostolic statement, *Evanglii Gaudium* was mostly a warning against the idolatry of money. (I–1) He cited evils of "unfettered capitalism," and "trickle-down" theory, which was not an attack of capitalism per se. However, Rush Limbaugh immediately slammed back, judging his official statement as "Pure Marxism."

Many statistics document a significant increase in US wealth disparity over the last 50 years. Since 1980, the top one percent of the population increased their share of the income by an astounding $1.1 trillion. Meanwhile, a fulltime wage was 11% lower in 2004 than in 1973, adjusted for inflation, even though productivity increased by 78%. Compared to other developed countries, only Mexico, Brazil and South Africa have greater wealth disparity than the US. Facilitated by big–money lobbying, more and more laws have been passed that help the rich at the expense of the poor. Some seem to think this judgment applies to the 2017 tax reform bill. Extreme wealth and disparity has been judged economically inefficient, politically corrosive, socially divisive, environmentally destructive, and unethical—but not inevitable. These judgments come from secular sources. Since the Bible is frequently cited for sexual aberrations that allegedly seriously threaten our moral and material future, the Bible should at least also be taken seriously for its wealth disparity concerns.

Just as in the time of Jesus and the prophets, discussion of economic morality is muted in our culture because of the power of money that may be withheld from organizations that depend on donor support. However, authentic prophetic messages were not popular in their own time. Opposition may be evidence of relevance, not something out of bounds. Such prophetic messages also fit with an authentic theology of the cross which, as noted previously, "calls a thing what it is" (see page 20). Theologies of glory are often reluctant to make such calls.

Government Ideologies and "Cliffs."

During the 2012 presidential campaign an opinion compared the economic options as choices between austerity and hope. A rebuttal letter preferred discipline vs. punishment. Without necessarily disagreeing with these views, I suggested the choice also was between ideology (Republican) vs. pragmatism (Democratic). (I-2)

I defined ideology as a mental formulation derived primarily from theoretical ideas, usually with broad application. In the case of economics, rigid concepts are considered applicable to all economies, whether robust vs. weak, or from health care delivery to all other goods and services. Part of this ideology is minimalist: minimal taxes, minimal fiscal regulation, minimal government, minimal teachers' compensation, minimal entitlements, or stimulus.

Pragmatism means policies supported by evidence from history or experience that are not necessarily the same for both sick and healthy economies. Although President Bush at first seemed against debt and his first Treasury Secretary, Paul O'Neal was, Cheney convinced Bush that "Reagan proved that deficits didn't matter," O'Neal was replaced. Cheney's "theory" was not well-grounded, the economy tanked and wealth disparity soared before his term was over. Rigid ideologies prevailed over morally framed, evidence-based thinking.

A guest opinion by a syndicated columnist speculated about what he regarded as the nation's next "cliff," which was thought likely to be much worse than the fiscal cliffs our congress is prone to bring us to. The pending cliff was regarded as not fiscal, however. Rather, it was "tyrannical," because of the government's evermore increasing control over personal lives through increasing taxes and regulations." (I-3) I suggested that another cliff the nation is at risk of facing is an integrity cliff.

A clearer understanding of this columnist's political philosophy was available from a web site where interviews done. He had the co-authored a book titled, "Free Market Revolution—How Ayn Rand's Ideas Can End Big Government." This approach was consistent with the "objectivism" political and economic philosophy of Ayn Rand (see pages 46–47). As noted, many theologians and others have judged her philosophy to be clearly anti–Christian.

Negative Criticisms

Some opinion letters attacked President Obama's personal integrity with unsubstantiated character allegations in the guise of policy disagreement. (I–4) One letter on economic issues alleged that President Obama had a hidden "true agenda" and a "mysterious force. . .greed for power." This was polarizing negative rhetoric, not constructive dialogue—the charge of a mysterious force of greed was pure hypothesis. The claim that Obama's agenda was for more equal wealth distribution was true, but it was false to allege that it was hidden. The general tenor of the letter was that for some people, it was bad enough to have a person like Obama elected president—worse yet if we all benefit from it.

Tax Returns and Tax Reform

A reader alleged that the failure of President Trump to show his tax returns was overblown because withholding them is not illegal. This stance ignored the reality that what is legal is not necessarily moral. The President dismissed concerns that he was hiding something that could make him emotionally distressed worrying that it would come to light. This could be a form of self-blackmail. (I–7)

The tax reform or tax reduction bill that was passed in December 2017 was estimated to increase the federal debt by $1.5 trillion dollars with most of the immediate benefits going to the wealthiest individuals and big corporations. (I–8) Relatively small tax reductions would go to the middle class with some theoretical benefits to the middle class in the distant future. The increase in debt is thought by some to become a future excuse for cutting Social Security and Medicare. A last-minute addition was a provision that would give windfall profits to big real estate owners. All these provisions seem to risk increasing wealth disparity more than reduce it, which morally is not consistent with biblical tenets. Time will tell, but in any case, the bill was significantly at odds with my prior formulation of biblical economic principles.

One appropriate summary of a biblical perspective on economics for current America is this three-word phrase that appeared a newspaper: "Prosperity trumps morality." A corollary to it could be: Immorality usually trumps prosperity. In any case, both Jesus and the Hebrew prophets warned that ill-gained prosperity is immoral, which usually undermines its longevity.

Summary

Ten of the twenty-one indictments of the prophets against Israel and Judah in Chapter 2 were about excessive wealth or disregard for cheating of the poor, and ten percent of Jesus' statements were about money and material matters ("mammon"). Economics are a big matter in biblical ethics. Theologians who write seriously about the meaning of these texts do not mince words: "Our society, like that of ancient Israel, is shot through with what Amos denounced: injustice and greed, pleasure loving ease, and venality." Opinions to which I responded included one whose author promoted Ayn Rand just as a current US Senator and House Representative have done. President Obama was criticized for wanting to redistribute wealth toward more equality, and President Trump was defended for not releasing his tax records. These views are hard to square with biblical emphasis. In the judgment of some reasonable analysts, the 2017 tax reform had parts that reflected greed rationalized more by hypothetical ideologies than sound economic principles. If true, a societal bill may risk coming due, as it did in the 2008 recession.

J. Foreign Policy

With Bible in One Hand

The Bible was written for contemporary and future believers by persons who did not conceive of a day when the faithful could be citizens of nations where a majority might be believers, have a right to vote, and hold elected offices. Therefore, like other aspects of governance, the Bible has no explicit guidelines on foreign policy for our time and circumstance. Some might argue this means the Bible is irrelevant. Another option extends principles articulated for believers on relationships in general, such as truthfulness, justice, and compassion. And again, or course, it is relevant to remember that God used presumed less godly nations to bring judgment on godlier Israel and Judah.

The next question is how this biblical record further relates to US foreign policy. An attempted answer will be formulated in three parts.

First, it seems important to recognize that, according to the Bible, God "allows" power of governing authorities for the sake of order "to punish those who do wrong and praise those who do right. (Romans 13:1 and 1 Peter 2:13) But governing requires some effort, integrity, and humility regarding the task: "Beware lest you say in your heart, 'My power and the might of my hand have gotten me this wealth'" (see page 32). You shall remember the Lord your God, for it is he who gives you wealth that he may confirm his covenant . . . Why do you go down to Egypt for help and horses without consulting the Lord?" (see page 24). "Remember, your ancestors who were slaves in Egypt, I brought them out." Some humility before God rather than some nationalistic bravado is called for with anyone who claims biblical faith.

Second, it seems fair to conclude that one of God's priority experiences is suffering and concern for those who suffer. War causes suffering, much of it on innocent non-combatants. God must hate war and Jesus said, "Blessed are the peacemakers." Therefore, peace treaties are a greater achievement biblically than winning a war.

Third, simple logic suggests that the biblical dictum "Righteousness exalts a nation but sin is a reproach to any people" is not only for how a nation deals with its own citizens, but also about how it deals with other nations. In WW-II, the US assumed the role of the world's super-power, which would place it in that special moral vulnerability category of being blinded by power to the point of globally abusing it. WW-II was one of the most morally justified foreign wars in its history because many nations were preemptively attacked and the actions of some of the enemies were unspeakably immoral. A case can be made that an attitude of superiority based on this perception has led to subsequent wars that have been unjust, and exceedingly costly. Lincoln's warning is worth repeating: " Many persons can stand much adversity. But if you want to test a man's character, give him power." The same can be said of nations.

Three foreign policy principles consistent with biblical principles are:

- Power alone does not make a nation great; rather, it is the wise and careful use of such power.

- Just war principles should rule when war becomes inevitable. War should be a last resort and not preemptive. Torture should not be used.

- National foreign policy should seek to have a reasonable balance between military "hard power" and the "soft power" of a robust State Department to vigorously pursue non-military solutions before resorting to war.

With Newspaper in One Hand

The issues of war, torture, terrorism, and refugees overlap foreign policy, but each issue was considered unique enough to deserve individual subject status. The following three opinions were considered primarily foreign policy.

The Syrian Dilemma

In 2013 when the Syrian situation was deteriorating, the Brainerd chapter of the Foreign Policy Association of the United States had a session of a video review followed by discussion on "The Syrian Dilemma." Because of some opinions referred to the issue, I reviewed some main points from that meeting. (J–1) The Great Decisions Program framed the issue as "Determining whether, when, where and why to intervene to protect civilians caught in the crosshairs of war and violence." This concept is usually labeled as the "responsibility to protect" (R2P)—to prevent, to react and to rebuild. The idea was that if any state is manifestly unable or unwilling to exercise the responsibility to protect its own citizens from mass murder, its sovereignty is abrogated. Along with this, other states have a responsibility to consider military intervention for humanitarian reasons.

The workbook essay summarized the Syrian problem as, "The responsibility to protect is a principle and not a tactic, and the principle remained intact in Syria even if international action was less forthcoming than in Libya . . . When governments resort to mass murder, we may have no easy solutions." Multiple risks of both deploying military forces and no military action were then discussed. A conclusion was that if the responsibility to protect concept has validity, it means, in the words of one author, "We are all atrocitarians now—but so far only in words and not yet in deeds."

Iran Nuclear Risks

During the negotiations leading up to the Iran Nuclear Agreement, I took exception to a letter that claimed a treaty with Iran would increase the threat of nuclear war more than a failed attempt would. (J–2) Contrary to the letter's implications, the treaty effort was not just an Obama-Kerry thing. All four of the other UN Security Council members (England, France, Russia, China) plus Germany are part of the negotiations. If a treaty then failed, both Israel and the US could become seriously alienated from some of these countries.

The anti-treaty argument also maintained that there should be tougher sanctions coordinated by the six nations and UN However, abolishing the treaty could cause all sanctions to come apart, especially since the US congressional majority preemptively stuck their finger in the eye of every coalition member. Therefore, the risk was that sanctions could end up far less stringent. If the treaty fails, Russia and possibly China could side with Iran against Israel, which could put the US against Russia on this issue. This would not bode well.

I concluded that a 10-year "breathing space" to test Iran's commitment under the close watch of inspectors is less risky than the risks without a treaty.

"God's Foreign Policy?"

A reader opinion letter titled, "God's Word is Clear On Israel." The letter made a Bible–deduced case for what the US policy stance should be regarding the Israel-Palestinian controversy. The opinion's recommendation was that there should be an undivided state of Israel against the common US—Israel common enemy, Islam-based terrorism. (J–3)

The alleged Scriptural basis for this stance was that the Old Testament covenant promise of giving the land to Abraham's descendants was the most ancient and unconditional right to the land of Palestine. (Genesis 17:7) I regarded this at best to be a partial truth. An alternate interpretation is that this promise to Abraham had been fulfilled in the Davidic state of Israel. The letter writer also did not note that the later (than Abraham)

Deuteronomy code regarding God's blessings vs. curses were prefaced with, "If you. . . do, or do not," obey. (Deuteronomy 28:1, 15) Furthermore, this Covenant was regarded by God as broken. (Jeremiah 31: 32) This judgment likely undermined previous covenants related to the land. At best, it should be accepted that the claim is disputed. To simply declare a single state of Israel as the only just outcome with no consideration of the methods of action and how just an outcome it is for Palestinians is not only dangerous, but a dangerous use of the Bible that undermines its moral credibility.

Foreign Policy Summary

The Bible outlines little that might be taken as foreign policy guidelines, except for a few passages such as this one from Isaiah: "Woe to you who go down to Egypt for help and rely on horses, who trust in horses because they are many . . . but do not consult the Lord." One derived principle, that of "Just War," should be certainly considered in the biblical tradition because of how it was elaborated on by Augustine and Aquinas. Even the Koran states that attacking first is preemption and should be avoided. It also logically follows that the "soft power" of "word" in diplomatic efforts to prevent war would be in the Christian tradition. Robust state departments would be expected to exist alongside of Defense Departments in governments that claim adherence to biblical principles. The Syrian issue started with a large component of "responsibility to protect" (R2P) that calls for international action when governments become unable to protect their own citizens. One reader's opinion stated that the risk of nuclear war was greater with an Iran treaty than with a failed treaty—a stance with which I disagreed.

Summary of Bible and Newspaper

Relevant biblical texts and principles may be found for most major news issues confronting the nation and smaller units of society. The overarching theme in relating the Bible to all life concerns is that the God revealed in the Bible is a moral being and with this revelation the Bible confronts a fallen world with a message that the well-being of any society over time will be related to what level of morality is attempted and /or achieved. Efforts and individual and societal morality should be done with the recognition that even with best efforts utopian perfection is beyond reach. Sin corrupts religion as well non–religious realities necessitating care to avoid Pharisaic self–righteousness at one extreme and moral tokenism at the other. Participation in government and public policy dialogue should be encouraged, keeping in mind the two–kingdom spiritual reality and the need for an arms'–length distance in speaking truth to power, along with reminders of power's corrupting nature. Linking alleged biblically derived policy stances with coercive government power always has dangers of perverting redemptive cross theology into perverse theologies of glory. Christians are called to be moral activists for health, justice, and peacemaking. They are called to be pacifists regarding violence. Focusing biblical religion excessively or only on afterlife concerns can compromise more than improve temporal life, and in some ways may compromise any hoped–for eternal welfare.

CHAPTER 4

American Christianity Since 1950

THE ENGAGEMENT OF THE moral dimensions of the Bible with major political issues has always in some sense been present in the US, although not always optimally Christian. In order to better understand some of the contemporary American context in which Christianity has engaged politics, this chapter will briefly review some trends since 1950. The information outlined is derived mostly from Putnam and Campbell's book, *American Grace: how religion unites and divides America.*[1] It should be noted that my selected references are a very small part of his comprehensive scholarly work. My understanding also comes partly from a three-day conference in 2014 at Luther Seminary on the "Spiritual but not religious" where the Putnam and Campbell book was cited frequently. Articles and opinions from a 2018 issue of *The Christian Century* informed an update on some themes in Campbell and Putnam's book (published in 2010).

Shocks and Aftershocks

Putnam and Campbell divide American religious history since World War II into three phases of a cultural shock. The first shock occurred in the 1960s followed by two aftershocks, one in the 1970s to 80s, and the other starting about 2000.

The US came through the Great Depression and WW II with a seemingly increased understanding of the importance of religion in life and culture, especially in the so-called Judeo-Christian traditions. These multiple traditions were different, largely based their different ethnic-historical

---

1. Putnam and Campbell, *American Grace. Bibliography*

origins. There was at least reasonable outward tolerance of the differences. But this cultural "Christendom" soon began to unravel in somewhat complicated ways.

The religious shock of the 1960s was caused by a perfect storm of multiple events: the baby-boomers moving through adolescence, the assassinations of the Kennedys and Martin Luther King, Jr., the Civil Rights Movement, and the Viet Nam War with its associated anti-war movement. The government Watergate scandal and the so-called death of God movement added to the disruptions. Yale Religious history professor Sydney Ahlstrom stated:

> The decade of the Sixties was, in short, when the old foundations of national confidence, patriotic idealism, moral traditionalism, and even of historic Judeo-Christian theism, were awash . . . It was perfectly clear to any reasonably observant American that the postwar revival of the Eisenhower years had completely sputtered out, and that the nation was experiencing a *crise de conscience* of unprecedented depth.[2]

Movements away from traditional denominations clearly began, some with Americans going to non-denominational "mega-churches," others to unchurched categories. One poll showed that the fraction of Americans who believed religion was "very important" dropped from 75 percent in 1952 to 52 percent in 1965. A survey of those who had dropped religious observances complained that, "The church was not playing its proper role in society—not keeping up with the times." One result, however, was that the evangelicals marshaled their forces in a counterattack, exemplified by the expansion of Campus Crusade for Christ from 109 employees in 1960 to 6500 in the mid 1970s.[3]

The First Aftershock

Putnam and Campbell designated the First Aftershock in the 1970s and 1980s as "The Rise of Religious Conservatism." The trend lines in American religiosity leveled off and began to climb somewhat during this time, but this trend was uneven. Most of the membership rise took place in non-denominational and evangelical churches. This rise was a little misleading

2. Ahlstrom, A Religious History of the American People, 1080–81, Bibliography

3. Putnam and Campbell, American Grace, 97–99, Bibliography

if measured against church attendance in that attendance per membership was some better in mainline churches, indicating their losses were more at their "fuzzy edges."

Factors noted in researching these phenomena raise some interesting questions. Pure "faith and fervor" comparisons may not be the whole story. For example, evangelicals tend to be much more literalist in interpreting the Bible than mainline denominations. For evangelicals, heaven, hell, and judgment day were realities, not metaphors, and moral issues were usually framed in absolute terms.

This rise in religious conservatism is explained by Putnam and Campbell in relationship to five main issues: Great Society liberalism, reaction to the civil rights movement, changing gender roles, Supreme Court decisions that widened separation of Church and State, and sexual permissiveness, especially regarding abortion and homosexuality. The sexuality issues seemed to overshadow all the others in significance. "Concern about sexuality was closely associated with the rise of evangelicalism."[4]

What I found interesting in this section of Putnam and Campbell's book is that except for abortion, few of the issues that I view as significantly moral in the twenty–first century were major issues in the 1960s or 1980s. This list includes health care, gun violence, preemptive wars, torture, refugees, global warming, and wealth disparity. In most of those years the NRA was focused on teaching gun safety, not marketing and politically lobbying for private weapon ownership. What I found a little surprising is that outside of mentioning the Viet Nam War once on the one page cited earlier, I did not find it mentioned again.

Certain sexuality issues became important in some Christian sectors. Having served in the US in the Army Medical Corps during the height of the Viet Nam war (1966–68), I observed that the lax morality represented by the Viet Nam War was a significant factor in the breakdown of marriage and sexuality norms. The Religious Right tried to blame this breakdown on the fledgling gay rights movement. But other observers thought the reality was the opposite: the hypocrisy of heterosexual promiscuity derived partly from cynicism over the War, plus the simultaneous scapegoating of homosexual persons spurred the gay rights movement. Princeton theologian William Stacy Johnson, in his book, *A Time to Embrace*, suggests this relationship:

4. Ibid., 114–119.

> What do we make of a society that whips itself into a frenzy over the prospect of gay marriage but greets the overwhelming evidence of torture by its leaders with a casual shrug of the shoulders . . . or when the subject is violence or warfare, they find flexibility and numerous alternative interpretations to the Sermon on the Mount's admonition to turn the other cheek"?[5]

In fairly affluent societies, there is evidence that immoral actions by governments erode moral sensibilities about sexual discipline and marital fidelity.

The Second Aftershock

The Second Aftershock noted by Putnam and Campbell that occurred in the 1990s and 2000s was labeled, "Youth Disaffection from Religion." A shift had taken place as demonstrated in a poll taken in the midst of the First Aftershock. With progressive evangelical Jimmy Carter on the ballot in 1980, twice as many evangelicals said his evangelical status had a positive effect on their vote.

By 1998, however, in response to the same question, a solid majority said they would be less likely to vote for such a candidate. This was after nearly a decade of publicity touting the Religious Right. "The terms 'Religious Right' and 'Christian Right' were becoming pejoratives for most Americans, as representing a "noxious mixture of religion and political ideology."

Christian fundamentalists were increasingly identified in the public mind with controversial causes, with "ideological intervention in politics binding evangelicals to the Republican Party."[6] Reactions to this included the view that religious leaders should not try to influence either people's votes or government decisions. Polls showed that this growing preference for separation of religion and politics was apparent in all parts of the religious spectrum.

Coincident with this was another quite striking phenomenon. When poll questions in the 1950s asked for religious preferences, only 3–5 percent responded by saying "none" or "nothing in particular." The rest named a religion or denomination. The "none" percentage then began to rise and by 2007 it was about 17 percent. It has since risen to about 25 percent (see page

5. Johnson, *A Time to Embrace*, 7. *Bibliography*

6. Putnam and Campbell, *American Grace*, 120–121. *Bibliography*

6). This trend lagged, but almost paralleled, the rise in persons responding that they did not attend any church worship services.[7]

Surveys showed that only a few of the nones claim to be atheists or agnostics. Most have some belief in God and even an afterlife and that religion is important in their lives. Some described themselves as "spiritual but not religious." Graphs of these trends showed that the rise of the new none's corresponded with a lag of about five years to the negative visibility of the Religious Right in the public media, "suggesting that the rise of the nones might be some sort of backlash against religious conservatism."[8] Conservatism may have tainted their view of Christianity as a whole.

A survey of the nones by the Pew Forum on Religion and Public Life asked why their rejection of organized religion was not theological or scientific. The answer was, "The new nones reported that they became unaffiliated, at least in part, because they think of religious people as hypocritical, judgmental or insincere. Large numbers also say they became unaffiliated (from churches) because they focus too much on rules and not enough on spirituality."[9]

One of the conclusions derived from this history of aftershocks was that, "In effect, the reach of evangelicalism is increasingly defined by the desire to convert conservative sexual morality into public policy." Furthermore, "It is also unsurprising that the increasing opposition to religious influence in politics and government . . . is heavily concentrated in the new nones."[10] This may be a partial explanation for why there is not much interest in addressing moral dimensions of major issues facing America in churches. It does not bode well for any attempts to do so.

Polarization, Sexuality, and Sermons

Putnam and Campbell's finding that probably relates most directly to the question of whether or not political dialogue is possible within congregations is that the shocks and aftershocks created a brand of polarization different from earlier denominationalism. As noted previously, in the 1950s and early 60s, there had been respectable tolerance, ecumenism, and acceptance of different religious views. The judgment of some is that

7. Ibid., 122, 123.

8. Ibid., 126–127.

9. Ibid., 131.

10. Ibid., 131.

what then transpired "left us with a noxious mix of religion and politics." What is "noxious" to outsider skeptics was not an inability on their part as outsiders to respect and tolerate different views, but rather the afore-mentioned "hypocritical, judgmental or insincere" attitudes that come with black and white, literalist, no-compromise absolutism that leads to that kind of religion. The politics of democracy requires compromise, and "no compromise" religion can compromise government functions. This new US Christian reality, whether intended or not, appeared to be at odds with most other US denominations. Putnam and Campbell therefore concluded that, "Religious polarization had increasingly aligned American's religions with their political inclinations."[11] Loyalty shifts to party over Christianity. This circumstance inhibits attempts for unity and constructive dialogue.

As noted above under the "First Aftershock," of the five issues that provoked the rise of the religious right, sexuality overshadowed all others. A few sexuality issues seemed to become litmus tests of both right practice and doctrinal belief. Ignoring the moral aspects of the full range of sexual misconducts together with disregard for the moral components of other major issues results in a selectively skewed morality. Once this moral frame-work is linked to one political party and its platform, it becomes judged in concert with all the actions its company keeps. The question up for debate is: Should a moral stance that adopts a primarily sexuality emphasis but stands for minimal restriction of firearms, minimal taxation of the rich, increasing wealth disparity, capital punishment, strict limits on refugees, exploitation of natural resources, while opposing health care for all and measures to curb global warming be judged as consistent with a holistic understanding of the Bible? (see pages 32–36). The answers we partisans may have to this question may be less relevant than those from skeptics and others defecting from biblical religions.

A necessary topic to consider before for considering political dialogue in any congregation is the acceptability vs. prohibition of incorporating politics into sermons. Putnam and Campbell address sermons several places in their book, but not related to the polarization in both politics and religion. I could also not find any consideration of the Johnson Amend-ment that prohibits church leaders from endorsing political candidates. Their observations and surveys do indicate that in general, parishioners do not want to hear any politics from the pulpit, and there usually is very little.

11. Ibid., 132.

That being said, one must acknowledge that defining what is vs. what is not political is somewhat ambiguous.

In reality, sermons that touch on hunger and poverty are relatively common, while sermons on wealth disparity are rare. In evangelical churches and Catholic churches, an average of about 72 percent of those surveyed heard sermons on abortion compared to 37 percent in mainline churches. There appears to be some selectivity in choosing issues without endorsing candidates, even though relevant differences among candidates may be well known. I see little wrong in keeping politics out of sermons if there is room for discussion of issues outside of worship services.

Negative perceptions of American Christianity

Most Americans who consider themselves nones, or spiritual but not religious, understandably view most the forgoing aspects of American Christianity negatively. American traditional expressions of Christianity, while always far from perfect, in recent decades seemed to be significantly more ineffective in maintaining a reasonably high level of moral consciousness, which is one of the primary functions of the church on the world it lives in. This reality, in turn, enhanced more than inhibited corrosive forces in American society as a whole.

Both liberal and conservative traditions show an inability to publicly and substantively make biblical faith relevantly engage most of the significant moral issues of the day. Often there seems to be a favorite few moral issues emphasized at the expense of the holistic ethic Jesus spoke of in Matthew 23:23: "Woe to you Scribes and Pharisees, hypocrites! For you tithe mint, dill, and cumin, and have neglected the weightier matters of the law: justice, mercy, and faith. It is these you ought to have practiced, without neglecting the others." But despite this, as noted in Chapter 3, in our time there have been some major theological voices raised in opposition to issues such as the preemptive invasion of Iraq, opportunity to universal health care at lower costs, and efforts to combat global warming. Unfortunately, such voices are often drowned out.

At the least, there could be more substantive and civil dialogue for the sake of the Americas and the world. The biblical statement that holistic moral clarity and practice "for your good" needs to be sounded loudly.

The Politics of Whiteness

The foregoing review of American Christianity between 1950 and 2010 outlined some facts and themes regarding the rise and subsequent leveling off or decline of what has been known as the American religious or evangelical right. Putnam and Campbell presented evidence that evangelicals felt "embattled," but they cited no evidence that other denominations or religions were deliberately attacking or in any way significantly criticizing them. The evangelical opposition was more to cultural shifts, some of them justice causes that evangelicals opposed.

There was, for example, resistance to the civil rights movement. Putnam and Campbell concluded that this was a smaller factor than sexuality issues. However, civil rights may have been a greater factor than was supposed. Of the five major issues that sparked the rise of the religious right, civil rights seemed at least a close second to sexuality issues.[12] This was not, however, a tightly knit conservative stance. Many evangelicals viewed a solid alignment with the Republican party as a deviation from basic biblical moorings. Most members seemed unaware of how their manner of mixing politics and faith was offensive to many observers, and may have contributed to the growing percentage of "nones" in the US.

A 2018 issue of *The Christian Century* had two editorials and two articles on the unexpected persistent strong evangelical support for President Trump despite his tarnished moral reputation. One article was titled "The Politics of Whiteness."[13] It first outlined the four traditional pillars of evangelicalism: the importance of conversion, vigorous activism in spreading the gospel, high regard for biblical authority, and the centrality of atonement. The author's view was that in this whiteness constellation, it is the whiteness, not sexuality, that is the centerpiece of evangelicalism. This is followed by abolition of legal abortion, gun rights, and low taxes (but not necessarily all in that order). This priority was very evident in the opposition to Muslim and other refugees seeking asylum in the US. The election of Barack Obama seemed to signal a need to fight for an America evangelicals once knew.

The author's corollary conclusion was that what distinguishes most evangelicals from most other Christians is politics, not theology. The biblical theological support for this whiteness constellation is not clear, but it

---

12. Ibid., 232–233, 389

13. Dowland, "The Politics of Whiteness?, 26–31.

is easier to understand in the context of Jim Crow segregation, a struggle against second wave feminism, and fears of a tyrannical federal government. [14.] Evangelicals also have a reputation of being the most reliable bloc of Republican voters. This puts evangelicals implicitly against universal health coverage, mitigation of global warming, and in favor of Ayn Rand's unfettered capitalism (see pages 46-50). Evangelicals also seem relatively anti-ecumenical—a factor that divides the biblical witness of American Christianity. This constellation has thus become a prominent face of white, American Christianity.

Frightened Christians

For evangelicals, the 2016 election was viewed against backdrop memories of their early growth when there was a sense that they could promote and implement what they thought America stood for. The election of President Obama made evangelicals feel marginalized and threatened. Their previous success seemed linked to a government relationship in controlling cultural issues to their liking. A sense of this "loss" created anxiety.

These dynamics were addressed in the same issue of *The Christian Century* cited in the previous section under the question of why conservative evangelicals showed such strong support for Donald Trump. One editorial noted that although there were many factors involved, one stood out above all others. This was a strong sense of fear. Somehow it seemed that many evangelicals had been sold on an ideology of fear that displaced a a disciplined life rooted in principles of faith. [15]

The Christian Century "The Editors" page quoted evangelical organizer Tony Perkins as stating that evangelicals were tired of being kicked around by liberals like Barack Obama. They were glad that finally someone was willing to fight back.

A feature article in the same issue of *The Christian Century* was titled "The Fear Sweepstakes." The first part was mostly a review of the Republican primary and presidential campaign. It noted that "What gave all candidates a legitimate shot at the nomination was their ability to engage in the politics of fear." The candidates knew that the faithful needed to be convinced that "the Christian fabric of the country was unraveling and ungodly immigrants were at the border ready to invade and take over. The contest came

14. Ibid., 31
15. Marty, "Hollowed Out by Fear," 3.

down to who could best convince the voters that they could protect the country from unworthy immigrants and the soft political correctness of the liberal media. [16] What the country seemed to need was not a person with top moral qualities, but rather an aggressive strongman.

Regarding any strongman assertions, *The Christian Century* editorial pointed out that Jesus' own message was not based on fear or resentment, nor did he seek worldly power for himself or his followers. Rather. he pointed to the creation of a society that includes everyone. Good stewards of the gospel would support efforts to that end by the same biblical standards in whatever society they live in.

But in contrast to this vision, in recent decades the evangelical right has taken on an identity of increasing fear toward ethnic and religious "others." This is difficult to understand, given the many assurances by both the Hebrew prophets and Jesus that faith creates a spirit to "Fear not:" or "not be anxious." Examples are Isaiah 43:1 ("Fear not, for I have redeemed you . . . "), and Matthew 6:31 and 10:31 ("Therefore do not be anxious . . . ." "Fear not . . . "). On the other hand, one might expect some concern about the scores of "Woe to you who . . . " warnings from the prophets and Jesus, but little such concern seems evident. A small sampling from the prophets is on pages 24–28 of chapter 2, The gospels also have dozens of similar "Woe to you" declarations from Jesus, including his "signature," "Woe to you . . . hypocrites! for you tithe . . . but have neglected . . . " (See pages 8–9, 54, and 105). In circles that claim the Bible is important, these admonitions seem worthy of equal attention on what we have to fear.

Summary

The "up" years for Christian churches in the US following World War II included the height of Billy Graham's evangelicalism, and general increased personal prosperity. This upbeat era came to a halt in the 1960s with the growing anti–segregation movement, the assassinations of the Kennedys and Martin Luther King, Jr. and disillusionment with the Viet Nam War. These factors caused interest in religion to wane and sexual promiscuity increase. Led by Jerry Falwell and others, this trend was countered with the formation of the Moral Majority, with its primary emphasis on family values linked to an anti–abortion stance in response to Roe vs. Wade, opposition to gay rights and birth control. This conservative movement became

16. Fea, "The Fear Sweepstakes," 22–25.

political, aligning itself squarely with the Republican Party. At the same time there was a gradual decline in the "mainstream middle" of American Christianity.

By the 1990s there was evidence of dissatisfaction with the religious right because of perceptions of the members being judgmental, hypocritical or insincere—a "noxious mixture" of religion and politics. Defections and decreased loyalty of younger members coincided with a corresponding rise in polls of a "none," or "spiritual but not religious" category of religion religious preference. Christianity became viewed as a more divisive than unifying element in American culture, including an aggravation of the divisive trend of political parties. A case can be made that the negative image of Christianity was less Christianity per se but a particular way it was expressed and it tainted all Christians.

In the last decades division of Christianity in American has been sharpened by the evangelical "right wing" becoming a sector known by its white identity, especially in its opposition to Muslim immigration and refugees seeking asylum. This has now likely become the identity of the Republican Party. This will not make civil dialogue over theological and socio-economic issues easier. These strands all seemed to come together in a "perfect storm" of the 2016 elections in which brazen anti–biblical standards were on full display. All of American Christianity may have been a loser in that election (A-11)

But all should not be considered lost. There are millions of Christians quietly and faithfully living upright lives going about their daily tasks according to their best understanding of biblical faith. And there are still paths available for positive change.

CHAPTER 5

"What Then Should We Do?"

The prophet Micah asked:

> With what shall I come before the Lord, and bow myself before the Lord most high?

> He has told you, O mortal, what is good; and what does the Lord require of you but to do justice, and to love kindness, and to walk humbly with your God?

Centuries later, as recorded in the third chapter of Luke's gospel, John the Baptist admonished his audience:

> Bear fruits worthy of repentance . . . " Some in a crowd then asked, "What then should we do?" John replied, "Whoever has two coats must share with anyone who has none, and whoever has food must do likewise." Even tax collectors came to be baptized, and they asked him, "Teacher, what should we do?" He said to them, "Collect no more than that prescribed for you." Soldiers also asked him, "And we, what should we do?" He said to them, "Do not extort money from anyone by threats or false accusation, and be satisfied with your wages.

Fruits worthy of repentance

To the question, "With what shall I come before the Lord?" the prophet Micah's answer designated broad themes of justice, mercy, and humility. John the Baptist's hearers asked similar questions, "What then shall we do?" John answered with admonitions for ethical actions that would be "fruits worthy of repentance." Ethical deeds are superior to words–only as evidence of authentic faith. It is worth noting that John's answers to the general question had a common theme: the affluent and powerful should not use their status to unjustly increase it at the expense of the poorer and weaker. One commentator on workingpreacher.org put it this way:

> John responds to each reiteration of this question by offering specific actions that translate into 'fruits worthy of repentance.' To the crowds as a whole, John says: *If you have more than you need, whether in terms of food or clothing, you must share.* To the tax collectors, who were often guilty of adding a little extra taxation on the top of regional and Roman taxes, John says: *Stop stealing from your neighbors.* And to the soldiers John says: *No more using your power to take advantage of simple citizens.* No hoarding, no skimming, no extortion (workingpreacher.org via index).

Broadly speaking, then, John's action-oriented fruits of repentance have to do with not depriving our neighbors of what they need. Repentance here is not only (or perhaps even primarily) about the dialectic of faith and sin; rather it is about how we are living out the love of our neighbor.

These ethical admonitions were given in the context of a society living under the harsh thumb of the Roman Empire, so all that citizens could do was to urge individual moral behavior according to just principles. The evidence is that for the three centuries of the Christian Church, most Christians did just that. And this is what helped its remarkable growth as a persecuted minority.

But this ethic needs translation into the context of a democratic society where all citizens have power to mold laws that best serve just principles. Public policies can allow one group to unjustly deprive neighbors living hundreds of miles away. For example, the US lower middle class had many families that lost their homes in the 2008 recession, not because of face–to–face extortion, but because of high risk mortgages and banks speculating with mortgage money. It requires public pressure and political activism to accomplish a reformed system compliant with biblical principles. But most Christian traditions live according to what Bonhoeffer defined as a two-sphere ethic. As one syndicated columnist put it, the church's primary responsibility is to help members become "fit for heaven." This relegates implementation of "Thy Kingdom come, on earth as it is in heaven" to a low priority.

Liturgical repentance

It should be acknowledged that the act of repentance happens frequently in Christian churches. The liturgies of many any denominations begin Sunday worship with a general confession of sin. In my tradition the standard version is:

> Most merciful God, we confess that we are captive to sin and cannot free ourselves. We have sinned against you in thought, word, and deed, by what we have done and what we have left undone. We have not loved you with our whole hearts; we have not loved our neighbors as ourselves. For the sake of your Son, Jesus Christ, forgive us, renew us, and lead us, so that we may delight in your will and walk in your ways, to the glory of your holy name, Amen.

The pastor then announces:

> Dear people of God, your sins are forgiven, In the great and abundant mercy of God, Jesus Christ was given to die for us, and for his sake God forgives us all our sins, giving us power to become children of God, set free to forgive others. In the name of the Father, and the Son, and the Holy Spirit, Amen.[1]

The rest of the worship service then follows.

The above tradition on the need for confession of moral failure might be considered important for intrinsic human moral weakness, especially considered in terms of individual piety. I have found the service very meaningful. It is a reminder of the need for humility, among other things. But this discipline does little to help the church or its members engage major issues unique to their time, such as those Barth and Bonhoeffer had to confront. I do not recall much specific instruction on this confessional liturgy, but I have always considered it a moment to reflect on the past week's personal events. I have often wondered if this confession was considered a time to repent for what some government action or policy had caused or was causing. In that context I could bring to mind my category list of biblical noncompliances. The list worthy of repentance could include the following:

Compared to most other advanced nations of the world:

- The US has failed to give adequate access to health care to all of its citizens.

---

1. ELCA, *Evangelical Lutheran Worship*, 212. *Bibliography*

- The US has failed to optimally control personal weapons to minimize injury and death from guns.

- The US has failed to eliminate racial disparities in equal justice and voting access.

- The US has failed to curb rising unhealthy wealth disparity among its citizens.

- The US has failed to grant refugee status to persons displaced by wars it has preemptively caused.

- The US has failed to keep an optimum balance between a strong State Department committed to diplomatic efforts to prevent war and the military weaponry to wage war.

- The US has failed to optimally minimize harmful gaseous emissions that aggravate global warming.

The above list of alleged failures is all outside of the direct purview Christian community discussion although there are likely connections some individual members have in vocations related to one of the issues. But there are theological issues directly involving the church. Is it reasonable to consider the above list as including some failures worthy of confessing before God? Dietrich Bonhoeffer was not reluctant to make such indictments of his church. In his *Ethics*, he has a section of over two pages in which he confesses on behalf of the church. Some excepts are:

> The Church confesses that she has not proclaimed often and clearly enough her message of the one God who has revealed Himself for all times in Jesus Christ and who suffers no other gods beside Himself. She confesses her evasiveness, her dangerous concessions. She has often been untrue to her office of guardianship and to her office of comfort. And through this she has often denied to the outcast and to the despised the compassion that she owes them. She was silent when she should have cried out because the blood of the innocent was crying aloud to heaven . . . She has stood by while violence and wrong were being committed under cover of God's name. The Church confesses that she has witnessed the lawless application of brutal force, the physical and spiritual suffering of countless innocent people, oppression, hatred, and murder, and she has not raised her voice on behalf of the victims. She

is guilty of the deaths of the weakest and most defenseless brothers of Jesus Christ.[2]

It doesn't take much reading between the lines to know what Bonhoeffer was likely referring to in these words, which it can be argued represent a night and day difference between his circumstance and those of the contemporary US. But it could be that a similar ambiguity about confessing failings existed in Germany at a time issues were not in such stark good vs. evil terms that caused the later Christian impotence. With that perspective in mind, the following theological issues related to this critique could be listed as possible failures.

- In Karl Barth's terms, American Christianity has allowed current events to influence moral/ethical interpretations of the Bible more than it has diligently attempted to broadly use the Bible to judge major issues and give witness to these judgments.

- A significant part of American Christianity may be tainted by what Barth described as unrecognized wrong belief or superstition.

- Martin Luther's understanding of the theology of the cross has been often corrupted toward patriotic and other versions theologies of glory camouflaged with retained cross imagery.

- The contemporary relevance of the Old Testament prophet warnings about the civil moral decay that occurred in Israel and Judah are mostly ignored by subverting the prophetic tradition primarily to predictions of a coming Messiah.

- Biblical stewardship is mostly practiced as a fall program to raise money for church operations rather than a holistic call to be God's good stewards of all life-relationships with Christ at the reconciling center.

- Ayn Rand's anti-religion and anti-government "virtue of selfishness" unfettered capitalism has been improperly melded with biblical themes implemented into risky policy by both politicians who know and who don't understand Rand.

- All these factors have conspired together to diminish the reputation of US Christianity, partially explaining the rise in recent decades of the "none" category of American religious preference.

2. Bonhoeffer, *Ethics*, 113–115. *Bibliography*

A valid criticism of the political and theological assertions enumerated above is that they are oversimplified, overstated and unopposed. This is, however, because they are set up as possible thoughts related both to liturgical confession and points for potential dialogue or debating propositions. This formulation also helps makes it seem possible that during a Sunday morning liturgical confession of sin a liberal oriented person could be smugly thinking of one side or list of issues and a conservative another, both in the same pew. It also points to a basic problem, which is an inability to have civil dialogue within the community. I doubt that many think that this will happen, and I suspect many would argue that it should not.

Some theologians have concluded that such resistance to "calling a thing what it is" is not unique to the US or the twenty-first century. It is endemic to the "Christendom" of the imperialistic West ever since Constantine in the fourth century. And to the extent that adhering more closely to an authentic theology of the cross that inhibits slippage into theologies of glory may be necessary for reforms into a more authentic Christian religion, Douglas John Hall warns that it was "never much loved." Authentic discipleship is not easy. In further explaining what he means by this, Hall writes:

> Perhaps for the present it will suffice to say that for a triumphant religion such as Western Christianity has been (and still, for the most part, wants to be), serious contemplation of such a tradition would involve a transvaluation of values so radical that the prospect of actually embodying them is discouraged from the outset. At least for the two northernmost countries of North America, it would be necessary, I think, to say that conventional Christianity needs to experience a greater failure than has yet befallen it before it is ready to discard the accumulated assumptions, beliefs, and practices of sixteen centuries of establishment and explore seriously such a radical alternative as is signaled by this tradition . . . Serious Christians know that they must either hearken to a different theological and missiological drumbeat or quietly concede to the forces of disintegration and decay.[3]

"Experience greater failure than has yet befallen it before it is ready . . ."? Shouldn't such a judgment about North American Christianity sound a bit shocking? Fifteen years after Professor Hall published this judgment, shouldn't we readily admit something is amiss and listen up? The lead

---

3. Hall, *The Cross in Context*, 15. *Bibliography*

first page article in the July 6, 2018, *Minneapolis Star Tribune* was titled, "As Churches Close, a way of Life Fades." Graphs showed how Minnesota mainline church membership has dropped about 25 percent since 2000 and the numbers of various denomination church closings were listed. National numbers were similar.

More than one observer has suggested that since the end of the Second World War, the US has developed a trajectory that deviated from a commonly perceived moral compass. That war was one of the most morally justified wars in US history in terms of being a response to unprovoked attack and some moral depravities of the enemy. But the resulting moral high ground seemed to give the US some unhealthy moral arrogance predisposing to multiple miss–steps, such as poorly justified preemptive wars. In any case, some respected theologians see further erosion of American Christianity and probably with it, societal deterioration.

The Donor Factor

Another concern is donor money. Evidence of this factor occasionally turns up on the press.

In early February 2017, a reader opinion in the Minneapolis *Star Tribune* asserted that the Johnson Amendment that prohibited churches from endorsing candidates had become an excuse for not discussing major moral issues in the church. Another reader's response suggested a more likely reason:

> This claim overlooked the history of the church as being a follower of social change, not a leader. The church cannot claim to have been leaders in the civil rights movement and it did not lead in the Vietnam demonstrations or the gay rights movement. There is a very good reason for the church's low profile in these cases, and it is a financial reason. What clergy want to upset a segment of their congregations for taking an unpopular stand? The members may speak with their feet and withdraw their financial support. Clergy have actually hidden behind the Johnson Amendment to avoid taking a stand on important social issues. Maintaining their tax-exempt status may also be a good reason for remaining silent on political-social issues.[4]

---

4. *Minneapolis Star Tribune*, opinion letter, Feb. 8, 2017.

Money concerns may affect messaging in our congregations much more than recognized or admitted.

Can Nothing Then Be Done?

A familiar Proverb (14:34) is: "Righteousness exalts a nation, but sin is a disgrace to any people." How can a nation's righteousness level be rated and trended? Christians are expected to live moral lives. But as has been noted, the Bible also speaks of levels of righteousness of nations below which God may seemingly affect history to bring such nations to their knees as a judgment for arrogant failings. In this context, a central question remains regarding what, if anything, can be done to make biblical "religion of the Book," and Christianity in particular, have a more positive moral effect on the US And how does one know when a line is crossed, as it was for the biblical prophets, such that the only message people of biblical faith are called to proclaim is that of an impending decline in societal well-being as a judgment from God?

After Isaiah said, "Here am I, send me," regarding the message that he was called to proclaim, he asked God, "How long, O Lord?" (Isaiah 6:11) It was as if he were asking how long it might take his hearers to repent. But the answer came back, "Until the cities lie waste without inhabitants. . and the land is utterly desolate." (Isaiah 6:1–13) The time for turning back had passed. No one can be sure of that point for any nation. But the question seems worthy of attention.

Is American Christianity so enamored by Adam Smith, Ayn Rand, and the almighty dollar that a public dialogue within its walls along the lines of Barth's Bible/Newspaper metaphor dare not be attempted? Is this our "Tower of Babel"? Are Americans like the monkey with his fist so tight in a grip on the peanut in a bottle that he can't remove his hand entrapped in it? Or is it simply that all nations, like humans, eventually ossify with age, and slide into decline?

What can be stated as a source of hope is that newspapers are a place in the public square where moral truth can be proclaimed like Nathan did to David. My view is that vigorous public exchanges with reasonable civility by ordinary citizens probably took place more often in the newspapers that I read regularly than at any other public venue. This is probably why Karl Barth held journalists in such high respect and had them high on his prayer list. Conversely, this function of the press explains why President Trump dislikes the press.

As repeatedly noted, however, the problem with newspapers as a venue for religion to affect public policy with a Barthian discipline is that there is not enough editorial space to have much impact. It would be much better if the Church could be making news with a united front of broad moral engagement. To do this the Church would have to become more of a forum for moral deliberation than it has been historically. If this cannot be done within its weekly programming, there would be a possibility of setting up a para-church auxiliary organization for this purpose. Unfortunately, both possibilities seem unlikely.

Fear of God

Given the barriers to change that seem to exist in American Christianity, perhaps all that is possible is some positive awakening among individual Christians. This change would be to agree to work toward becoming more outwardly God-fearing. This chapter will close with a different possibility that all individual American Christians can work toward that might counterbalance the American political leadership failures. This change would be to agree becoming more authentically God-fearing. This theme allows all of the other biblical themes used in this book to operate, even if less effective in division rather if unified. Such a less visible group could constitute what the Bible many times refers to as a remnant: "A remnant will return, the remnant of Jacob, to the mighty God. For though your people Israel be as the sand of the sea, only a remnant of them will return . . . Then shall come forth a shoot from the stump of Jesse, and a branch shall grow out of his roots . . . and his delight shall be in the fear of the Lord." (Isaiah 10:21, 11:1).

"Fear of God" or "fear of the Lord" is a notion that seems to get relatively little theological attention. But attention to it could give some insight into the decline of Christian impact on overall American societal morality. A logical explanation for neglect of God-fearing emphasis is that superficially it seems to give an image of God that is more coercive than loving. This reasoning is based on a misunderstanding of what constitutes biblical fear of God.

My confirmation instruction involved a lot of memorization of Martin Luther's *Small Catechism*: Question: What is the First Commandment?"

Answer: "You shall have no other God's before me." Question: "What does this mean?" Answer: "We should *fear*, love and trust God above all things" (italic emphasis added). Answers to the "What does this mean? Questions for all other commandments begins with the same words: "We should fear and love God in order that we . . . " These words have been indelibly etched into my consciousness in creating more a sense of reverence than a negative sense of fear.

My view of the fear of God is not the terror of facing a tiger or a rattle-snake. It is better described as reverential awe. It has been likened to a fear of carelessly offending or hurting someone loved very much, especially if there is a fear of losing a valued relationship. It has been suggested that what galvanized Jesus' disciples into such effective post–Easter witnesses was partly the pain they experienced after scattering like frightened sheep after his arrest. Their fear was a positive motivation to not miss opportunities to express love as gratitude for love experienced, not fear of some other punishment.

Fear of God in the Bible

Some biblical facts make Christian disinterest in the concept of God–fearing seem misplaced. According to one Bible Concordance, the phrase "Fear of God" in one form or another occurs over 100 times in the Old Testament and about twenty times in the New Testament. It is not that rare. An interesting related fact is that the phrase, "Fear not," spoken by God directly, through a prophet, an angel, or by Jesus, is found fifty–two times in the Old Testament, and fourteen times in the New Testament. A relationship seems to exist such that those who fear God have less need to fear all else. Conversely, those who do not fear God, have more to really fear.

Genesis 15 begins with God in a vision saying, "*Fear not* Abram, I am your shield, your reward will be great." Later, in reference to a region in which he was sojourning, Abraham told Abimelech, "There is no *fear of God* in this place, and they will kill me because of my wife." In chapter 22, an angel appears to Abraham and said, "Do not lay your hand on the lad, or do anything to him; for now I see that you *fear God* . . . " All three of these events were long before there were the ten commandments, but the texts show that some good vs. evil relationship is linked with fear of God.

Other passages link this fear with increased wisdom, knowledge, and blessing. In Psalms 111 and Proverbs 9 is the counsel "The *fear of the Lord* is the beginning of wisdom." A passage thought to be a prediction of Jesus (a shoot from the stem of Jesse) indicates the Messiah would have "the spirit of knowledge and *fear of the Lord.*" (Isaiah 11:1–3) In the first chapter of Luke, Mary praises God: with "My soul magnifies the Lord, and my spirit rejoices in God my Savior . . . his mercy is on *those who fear him*, from generation to generation." (Luke 1:50)

How does one best describe a person who fears the God as outlined above? A good starting point could be one that fits Micah's description at the beginning of this chapter: "Do justice, love mercy, and walk humbly with your God." Biblical fear, as noted for this discussion, is linked to love received and love wanting to be gratefully returned. This awareness creates a spirit of humility instead of arrogance and seeks to do justice with mercy. Such is a person who fears God.

Soren Kierkegaard

A major Lutheran theologian who did not shy away from the biblical theme of fear of God was Soren Kierkegaard. In 1843, a book by Kierkegaard was published in Denmark titled, *Fear and Trembling*, a phrase also found several times in the New Testament.[5] I certainly do not claim to be any authority on Kierkegaard's mixture of biblical theology and philosophy, which some find controversial. But some of his ideas seem relevant to understanding the biblical meaning of fear of God. Douglas John Hall also includes Kierkegaard in a list of theologians that were knowledgeable about and advocates of Luther's theology of the cross.

Kierkegaard thought that Christianity in Denmark at his time was meaningless for most people. He boldly argued in print for more serious biblical thinking. A short summary of some of Kierkegaard's theology will attempt to explain some relevance to faith and repentance.

Kierkegaard exposed how many in his day thought that they could easily understand and explain faith, hope, and love components of spiritual life. He demonstrated that although they could verbalize faith as a concept, they added little to understanding or evidence of growth and how to achieve it. In addition, Kierkegaard noted that the Danes of 1850 thought that it had reached the "highest attainment" of Christian faith. He countered that one generation cannot pass on greater understanding and depth that can help the next generation achieve stronger faith. All persons in every generation

5. Kierkegaard, *Fear and Trembling. Bibliography*

start at the same point and must make the best possible out of what they experience: "No generation has learned from another how to love, no other generation begins at any other point in love than the beginning . . . There are perhaps many in every generation who do not reach it, but no one goes further than someone else has."[6]

Kierkegaard uses Abraham, a pioneer example of faith (Hebrews 11:8–19), to help clarify his own view of faith. The most important example in Abraham's life was his willingness to obey God's instructions to sacrifice Isaac, his only son. Kierkegaard can only say he admires Abraham—but he cannot say he understands him regarding what must have been such a tortuous experience. Apparently this was not so in the "System" of theology in Denmark at the time. Kierkegaard described how the Abraham story had been construed another way:

> They extol God's grace in bestowing Isaac on him again—the whole thing was only a trial—over as quickly as it is said. One mounts a winged horse, the next instant is at Mount Moriah, the same instant one sees the ram; one forgets that Abraham rode only on an ass, which walks slowly along the road, that he had a journey of three days, that he needed some time to cleave the wood, to bind Isaac, and to sharpen the knife."[7]

No, Kierkegaard suggests, we all would prefer to glibly dismiss this story as "only a trial." It is as if there was "no history of dread."

> If a man does not have enough passion to make one move or the other (regarding faith), if he loiters through life *repenting a little,* and thinks the rest will take care of itself, he has once and for all renounced the effort to live in the idea . . . to delude himself and others with the notion that in the world of the spirit everything goes as in a well-known game of cards where everything depends on haphazard (italics emphasis added).[8]

But most persons may not be as far from the reality of more authentic faith as they think:

> One generation does not improve understanding or pass on how to experience faith better. In those old days it was different, the task of faith was for a whole lifetime, because it was assumed that

6. Ibid., 131–32.

7. Ibid., 62–63.

8. Ibid., 109.

the dexterity of faith was not acquired in a few days or weeks. When the tired oldster drew near to his last hour, having fought the good fight and kept the faith, his heart was still young enough to not have forgotten that *fear and trembling* which chastened the youth, which the man indeed held in check, but which no man quite outgrows . . . "[9]

How many of us easily remember the first times as a child that we contemplated what this concept of God meant? Might we have experienced some *fear and trembling* that is now mostly in the subconscious—which no one quite outgrows?

In the second chapter of Philippians Paul begins what is known as the Christ Hymn with the words, "Have this mind among yourselves, which you have in Christ Jesus . . . " After the end of that paragraph he adds: "Therefore, my beloved, as you have always obeyed, so now, not only as in my presence but much more in my absence, work out your own salvation with *fear and trembling;* for God is at work in you, both to will and to work for his good pleasure. (Philippians 2:5–7) Some commentators have noted that this "work out" language has been routinely troublesome for Protestants, who fear it implies a form of "works righteousness." But they note that Paul's focus here has nothing to do with salvation. Instead, Paul is concerned with how "saved" (believing) people *live out* their salvation *here and now in the world.* And these are matters of obedience, humility, and public witness.

Conclusion

The above brief reference to Kierkegaard's interest in fear and trembling is background for concluding with a short prayer–meditation from another of his books:

> *Knowing then what the fear of the Lord means, we endeavor to win men.* (2 Corinthians 5:11).

To begin at once or first of all to wish to win men may even be ungodliness; in every instance, it is worldliness and no more Christianity than it is fearing God. No, let your endeavor—let it first and foremost—express that you fear God. This I have tried to do.

9. Ibid., 23.

But Thou, O God, Thou lettest me never forget that even if I did not win a single man, if my life (for the protestation of the lips is deceitful!) expresses that I fear Thee, *All is won!* On the other hand, if I won all men, if my life (for the protestation of the lips is deceitful!) does not express that I fear Thee, *All is lost!*[10]

Perhaps it is totally unrealistic to hope that American Christians can unify in ways that facilitate dialogue over ethical dimensions of multiple major issues leading to policy recommendations. But what can be done is to promote life disciplines that witness to an authentic fear of God such that God may "save" the nation from otherwise disastrous consequences.

10. Kierkegaard, *For Self-Examination*, ii (preface), *Bibliography*

Postscript

Trumpism

Enter Donald Trump

A SIMPLE DEFINITION OF Trumpism is the philosophy and politics of Donald Trump. I have found other definitions of Trumpism that include other "isms" such as nationalism, nativism, protectionism, populism, etc. However, for a critique in a moral biblical context I prefer a definition that includes the word politics because it signifies that Trump's success was dependent in significant part on the American electorate that largely discounted his several unbiblical character traits. In so far as Trumpism is a philosophy, it is not entirely new in American life, and it has been identified with a number of negative "isms" in American history.

What seems unique in Trumpism is its strong support by a segment of American Christianity while at the same time President Trump disregards the broad ethical–moral framework of the Bible. The biblical theme of this book is the assertion that God is a moral being and the long–term well–being of any earthly society will be ultimately proportional to its levels of awareness and adherence to the Bible's broad moral prescriptions. Similar claims are found in other religions and intellectual philosophical systems. Some countries may appear to be outwardly less interested in the Bible, but their overall conduct may better match the Bible than groups that claim strong biblical adherence. This postscript examines these relationships to Trumpism.

Despite the seeming lack of biblical morality in Trumpism, only scant reference has been made to President Trump's election thus far in this book. In addition, his candidacy and time in office are critiqued as a postscript rather than a chapter. This placement is partly to emphasize that my moral political stance was formulated long before Trump became a candidate for president, and it was not in response to it. This reality is reflected in the fact that about eighty percent of my opinions were published before Trump was nominated as a candidate—none about him were published before. My plans for analysis and possible publication of my thesis would not have changed if Hilary Clinton had been elected President.

Another reason for the postscript placement is that some of President Trump's media obsessions, policy stances, and disregard for ethical norms distract from the nuances and usual civil give and take in most of life and politics. Mixing this too much with Trump's entrance could detract from the main purpose of this analysis. On the other hand, Trumpism presents a unique ethical challenge deserving of consideration. This attention will begin with Trump's policy stances in the ten category subjects, followed by a focus on personal character and major ethical issues.

In explaining this arrangement, it seems relevant to repeat what was stated in chapter 1 about how I view President Trump's relationship to my project, if we may call it that: Trump entered into a scheme not designed because of him, but unintentionally readymade to facilitate making some comparative judgments about him.

With respect to objective policy comparisons, my conclusion is simply that President Trump is more the polar opposite of my positions in all ten subject categories than almost any candidate for president in the 2016 election, both Republican and Democrat. It does not seem necessary to run through each category to demonstrate why his judgment is reasonable. To the extent that my policy stances on health care, gun violence, global warming, etc., are judged to be the more biblical of options, it would follow that Trump's positions on such issues are not only markedly different from mine, but more more different from those of most Republicans.

With regard to the category of personal morality, President Trump's relationship to organized Christianity seems at best ambiguous. He claims to be a Presbyterian Christian. But when asked once if he ever felt a need to confess wrong–doing, his response was that he didn't think his errors were bad enough to warrant confessing them as sins. He explained that he simply corrected the behavior. Trump seems to have no recognition or appreciation of universal human traits of selfishness and egocentricity competing with desires to be generous and compassionate.

Unlike President Obama, who could converse with journalists about Reinhold Niebuhr on government policy, I have never heard President Trump quote any theologians. The only time I heard him quote the Bible was in his noted citation from "Two Corinthians" in an address at Liberty University that suggested little past study and conversation about the Bible. One is left with the feeling Trump has little appreciation for theological concepts such as living in two realms or under what it means to live with a reverent fear of God. His economic theory seems close to that of atheist Ayn Rand (see page 47), even though he may not recognize this.

Part of President Trump's uniqueness is that moral considerations— as distinguished from legal—seem virtually absent in most of his policy discussions and positions. He seems to dismiss the concept of conflicts of interest. He found no ethical need to reveal his recent tax returns but he wanted transparency from the Special Counsel. Trump's reformed stance on abortion might be considered a significant moral sexuality stance. But this could be Machiavellian convenience that comes with many allegations and an admission of sexual harassment. Abortion in this context can serve as a moral linchpin that substitutes for or justifies absence of moral concern on other major issues. If the abortion pin is pulled, there is only a thin morality.

The Bible rejects substitution ethics: "Woe to you . . . for you tithe mint and dill and cumin and have neglected the weightier matters of the law, justice and mercy and faith; these you ought to have done without neglecting the others" (Matthew 23:23). Such formulations may also represent what Barth designates as wrong religion, religious superstition, or the improper use of newsworthy issues to affect biblical interpretation rather than the opposite.

The "Successful Man."

What surprised me about the Trump phenomenon was not that many Americans would buy into his candidacy, but I expected it to still be a substantial minority. It may be granted that Trump did a masterful job of tapping into the fears and grievances of many Americans. It may be that he has also been a rhetorical "master manipulator" in using the existing media to keep his name at the forefront. But my judgment had been that there were plenty of red flags to indicate that his promises and plans for the nation were riskier than average. His psychological status is a separate question that I will not address.

One perspective from which to address the question of why the American electorate turned toward President Trump or had independently

changed enough to elect him, is to consider the relevance of a section of
Dietrich Bonhoeffer's unfinished *Ethics* titled, "The Successful Man." Some
of Bonhoeffer's exact words are worth noting:

> In a world where success is the measure and justification of all
> things the figure of him who was sentenced and crucified remains
> a stranger and is at best an object of pity. The world will allow
> itself to be subdued only by success. In this worldly concept, it
> is not ideas or opinions, which decide, but deeds. Success alone
> justifies wrongs done. Success heals the wounds of guilt . . . [but]
> No indictment can make good the guilt which the successful man
> leaves behind him . . . With a frankness and offhandedness which
> no other earthly power could permit itself, history appeals to its
> own cause the dictum that the end justifies the means.

> When a successful man becomes especially prominent and con-
> spicuous, the majority of citizens give way to the idolization of
> success. They become blind to right and wrong, truth and untruth,
> fair play and foul play. They have eyes only for the successful deed,
> for the successful result. The moral and intellectual critical fac-
> ulties are blunted. It is dazzled by the brilliance of the successful
> man and by the longing to share in his success. It is not even seen
> that success is healing the wounds of guilt, for the guilt itself is no
> longer recognized. Success is simply identified as the good. This
> attitude is genuine and pardonable only in a state of intoxication.
> When sobriety returns, it can be achieved only at the price of an
> inner untruthfulness and conscious self-deception. This brings
> an inward rottenness from which there is scarcely a possibility of
> recovery . . . And if success is the measure of all things, it makes
> no essential difference whether it is so in a positive or a negative
> sense.

> The figure of the crucified invalidates all thought which takes suc-
> cess for its standard. Such thought is a denial of eternal justice.
> Neither the triumph of the successful man nor the bitter hatred
> that the successful arouse in the unsuccessful can ultimately
> overcome the world. Jesus is certainly no apologist for the suc-
> cessful men in history, but neither does he head the insurrection
> of shipwrecked existences against their successful rivals. He is not
> concerned with success or failure, but with the willing acceptance
> of God's judgment (of both the successful and unsuccessful) . . . It
> is a sentence of mercy that God pronounces on mankind in Christ
> . . . It was precisely the cross of Christ in the world, which led to his

success in history . . . Only with this judgment is there reconciliation among men. It is the sentence of mercy that God pronounces on mankind in Christ.[1]

Several points in this citation deserve special note. First, Bonhoeffer was not faulting all successful persons. The "worldly" kingdoms he referred to include some with an ethic of "the end justifies the means." The "end" of "success" that Bonhoeffer is referring to above allows an unethical "means" to achieve it. In this case it included "wrongs done" . . . causing "wounds of guilt." Clearly the "means" Bonhoeffer was referring to were significantly unethical. Success achieved in this way indicates some moral sickness.

Second, the effect unethical success has on the majority of citizens is negative: "When a successful man becomes especially prominent and conspicuous, the majority of citizens give way to the idolization of success. They become blind to right and wrong, truth and untruth, fair play and foul play."

Third, this negative phenomenon of these worldly kingdoms is "invalidated" by "the figure of the crucified," representing the alternate kingdom of moral reality. This kingdom's judgment not only identifies the other's rottenness and eventual demise, but points to an alternate path to avoid negative outcomes. It starts with the necessity of accepting God's judgment about human sin and the path of dealing with it, elsewhere called the gospel.

Bonhoeffer likely had Hitler in mind in this "successful man" designation, but perhaps for self-protection security reasons he didn't dare make that identity explicit. The challenge for our day is to understand how ethical concepts are easily corrupted in political contexts. Again, personal success per se is not unethical. But how success is attained and/or how it is used can be unethical. And short-term unethical apparent success risks undermining long-term outcomes.

The obvious relevance of Bonhoeffer's "successful man" warning is whether or not President Trump qualifies enough to explain at least part of his political success. This connection is in no way an attempt to suggest Trump is anything comparable to Hitler. Although Trump has liabilities, the issue here is whether or not for voters his business success overshadowed ethical concerns that would otherwise sideline less economically successful persons.

The focus of this Bonhoeffer perspective is as much on trying to understand those who voted for Trump as it is in understanding him. It seems

1. Bonhoeffer, *Ethics*, 75–78. *Bibliography*

fair to state that President Trump would likely not have been as viable a candidate had he not been a billionaire.

Opinion letters regarding President Trump

My opinion letters with some reference to President Trump touched relatively little of what could have been written about his differences with my stances. This was partly because I maintained my self-imposed schedule of writing an average of one opinion per month, which included at least as many with no reference to him. This was appropriate because Trump was an addition to my project and not its occasion. On the other hand, even these relatively few letter–length opinions cover a range of major moral issues that Trump represented. This will be documented using two complete original letters and reference only by title to eight others. The first two complete opinions were written between Trump's nomination and his installation as President. The italicized phrases indicate different moral issues.

Moral Issus in Two Opinions

Smokescreen Biblical Morality (10–18–16)

A September 29 Dispatch letter warned of God's judgment on the US for human disobedience, citing only "*the sin of* homosexuality." The next week, a guest opinion by syndicated columnist Cal Thomas provided a similar view of homosexuality *and abortion.* Together, these opinions referenced these sins to the *religious faith of candidates.* Tim Kaine, Hillary Clinton, and Mike Pence. Trump was not mentioned.

These opinions reflect the limited morality of the Tea Party/religious right coalition that uses these two *issues as a smokescreen* that hides an apparent inability to find biblical relevance to most other major issues facing the nation. These issues include health care reform, marketplace fraud, increasing wealth disparity, unfettered capitalism, global warming, gun violence, preemptive war, torture, refugees, and immigration.

This analysis is supported by fact that heterosexual assault of women was given little campaign attention until the audio-video that hit the news on October 7 documenting thrice-married Trump *bragging about the sexual assault behavior* he could get by with. Multiple women bravely come forward to contradict Trump's assault-denial. He and his supporters argue that his denial should be believed even after his five-year fraudulent *Obama-birther campaign.*

Unfortunately, the Republican Party has been tarnished by Trump, with Trump defenders now gamely attempting to morally explain their continuing support of him. Their main comparison is Bill Clinton, who was punished with impeachment. Trump's apologists argue that his angry apology deserves Bible-based forgiveness with no adverse consequences. This *skewed version* of Christianity will likely have negative effects long after the election. Care should be taken in judging the reasons for God's judgments.

An Election Loser? (1–5-17)

The title of a recent *New York Times* guest editorial by noted progressive evangelicals Tony Campolo and Shane Claiborne was: "The Evangelicalism of Old White Men is Dead."

Campolo and Claiborne observed that beginning in the 1980s, the religious right made a concerted effort to align evangelicalism with the Republican Party. By the mid '90s, *the word evangelical had lost its positive connotations* with many Americans who came to see Christians—and evangelicals in particular as anti–women, anti–gay, anti–environment, anti–immigrant and champions of guns and war. For these evangelicals, Trump's victory victory "pulled the roof off the building" they once called home."

Donald Trump's view of his life-relationships beyond family seems to follow the dictum that *"Money is the measure of all things,"* with an associated ethic that *the end-justifies-the-means. Long* before Trump the candidate, evangelicals took upon themselves the mantel of the leaders and measure of authentic Christianity in the US. But exit polls showed that fifty percent of evangelicals that were expected to vote for Senator Cruz voted for Trump, and eighty percent voted for him in the general election. This, when there is hardly a word or action of Jesus that easily squares with Trump's.

The *credibility and prevalence of Christianity* in the U.S. may be diminished by the election of Donald Trump. But this doesn't mean the existence of biblical faith is dependent on US biblical faithfulness. If God is in charge, as some Dispatch reader-letters like to assert, it means God can tilt the nation's trajectory in either a positive or negative direction.

We should all pray for peace and prosperity under our President-elect. But the electorate has rejected many other candidates to put its stamp of approval on the one whose life-testimony seems *the most unbiblical.* There are biblical reasons this should cause some unease.

The moral issues in these two opinions are:

1. Controversy over abortion and homosexuality as major moral sins.

2. Limited sexuality morality as "cover" for lack of moral considerations on other issues.

3. Sexual assault not usually cited as a significant moral concern.

4. Trump's five-year span of false claims regarding President Obama's birthplace.

5. Republican Party tarnished by Trump's audio–video tape admissions.

6. Negative implications of word "evangelical" worsened by Trump election.

7. Trumpism as "money is the measure of all things"—similarity with Ayn Rand.

8. The only Trumpism ethic seems to be the end–justifies–the–means.

9. The credibility of all US Christianity may be diminished by Trumpism.

10. Many US Christians supported the arguably most unbiblical candidate.

Moral Issues in Other Trump Opinions

11. *Deceptive Questions* (8/12/16): Stereotyping all Muslims as equal risk.

12. *Obamacare Repeal* (2/16/17): Promises of better health plan but unable to create one.

13. *Tax Return Transparency* (5/10/17): Legal arguments without ethical considerations. What is Trump hiding?

14. *Muslim Ban Orders* (5/26/17): Muslim bans are unbiblical and dubiously constitutional.

15. *Back to the Bible?* (10/19/17).—with military increase but State Department decrease?

16. *Shameless Greed* (12/29/17). Tax reform disproportionately benefits the rich while increasing debt.

17. *Anti–DACA Family Values* (1/10/18). Broken promise to DACA immigrants.

18. Lost Children (5/30/18) "Malevolent incompetence" at the border.

The above list touched all of the ten subject categories in this critique except gun violence and global warming. However, President Trump had declared stances that are also at obvious odds with my stance on those issues. In one of the above opinions I suggested that despite my differences I thought we should pray for Trump's success. However, I didn't reveal my ambivalence in making this statement related to the reality that success, if accomplished by unethical means, encourages more of the same. This in turn can lead to even worse future failures. The risk in this gambling gambit gets high at the national level. The best prayer to God for many Trump ventures might therefore be, "Thy will be done."

President Trump's disregard for truth was hardly touched upon in my opinions. This may be a sign that his troubled relationship with truth is not only "normal" for President Trump, but increasingly the "new normal" for more Americans. Biblically, one can argue that this should be of concern regarding America's future: "Truth has fallen in the public square (Isaiah 59:14); "Falsehood and not truth has grown strong in the land. (Jeremiah 8:22); "They abhor him who speaks the truth." (Amos 5:10) Jesus told Pilate: "I have come into this world to bear witness to the truth. Everyone who is of the truth hears my voice," implying those who are not "of the truth" will not likely honor all Jesus says. (John 18:37) Pilate responded to this with his trade mark sneer: "What is truth?" (see Niebuhr, chapter 2).

President Trump's difficulty with truth has a corollary in an inability or unwillingness to recognize wrong-doings and apologize for them. Paul admonished: "Therefore, putting away falsehood, let everyone speak the truth with his neighbor." (Ephesians 4:25) Jesus said, "Go first and be reconciled with your brother . . . " (Matthew 5:24)

President Trump also doesn't recognize or discards the biblical principle of human decency "Let your speech always be gracious, seasoned with salt . . . " (Colossians 4:5) "All things should be done decently and in order." (1 Corinthians 14:40; see also page 80 and original opinion F–6: "Religion Kills—So Does Sarcasm," page 166) If the counter argument is that these words were meant only for church relationships, this reasoning displays a double standard two–sphere ethic over the better one–sphere.

President Trump's relationship to truth in regard to science also seems to be more in the realm of selective personal opinion than objective facts. Once science moves from proposition or theory to consensus, this usually means the conclusion stands as fact. Most of the educated world has accepted the reality of global warming to be actionable enough for policy. "Conservative" used to mean prudence about the future— "conserve" what is of value—and not just money. It promoted the long view. But now short–term profit at the expense of the national debt is the alternative new conservative reality. Trump pulled the US out of the Paris Climate Accord, which will likely become an even more embarrassment in the future.

President Trump's Moral Epitome

Some credible insights into the President's larger ethical vision were suggested in a June 2, 2017, commentary in the *New York Times* by conservative columnist David Brooks. Brooks' essay was mostly a commentary on one sentence in an opinion in the *Wall Street Journal* written by two of President Trump's top advisors, H.R. McMaster and Gary Cohn: "The president embarked on his first foreign trip with a clear-eyed outlook that the world is not a 'global community' but an arena where nations, nongovernmental actors and businesses engage and compete for advantage."

Brooks regarded this sentence as a description of the epitome of the Trump philosophy—selfishness is the sole driver of human affairs. Life boils down to a competitive struggle for control. Cooperative communities are hypocritical covers for selfish posturing underneath. "Morality has nothing to do with anything . . . everything is about self–interest." It explains why Trumpism wants to pull out of treaties and the Paris climate accord.[2] Note

2. Brooks, "Donald Trump Poisons the World," *New York Times,* editorial.

the critical role of selfishness, similar to the title of Ayn Rand's republished essays, *The Virtue of Selfishness* (see page 47).

Brooks acknowledges that people are driven by selfishness, but that is not the half of it. Most persons are also driven by urges for solidarity, love, and moral fulfillment that at times are more powerful than selfish impulses. Most people have a moral sense and are wired to cooperate. Children do not have to be taught about what fairness is. People feel disgust with injustice and greed and reverence for excellence, goodness, and the sacred. It is much easier to destroy bridges than build them.

Brooks' description fits both the way President Trump deals with individual relationships and how he thinks the US should deal with other nations. One moves up in the world primarily by subduing others—the alleged best way to make America great again.

Christianity and Trumpism

The part of the Christian electorate that supported President Trump and most helped him win the election was the evangelicals, referring here especially to those led by names such as Dobson, Falwell, Robertson, and Graham. Eighty percent of these white, self–identified evangelicals voted for Trump, and that level of support remained through his first year in office. But as noted already, evangelicals like Tony Campolo and Shane Claiborne strongly opposed Trump. The question arises as to whether this Trump–related division among evangelical Christians may have spread to taint all American Christianity into a 2016 election loser in terms of societal credibility. This in turn could accelerate the trend of younger generations becoming "nones" rather than Christians. (A–11, see also pages 6, 102–3)

Television commentary programs during the 2016 campaigns had Trump–defender panel members on cable TV programs justify their support with arguments such as, "If God could use the harlot Rahab for the good of his people, God could certainly use Trump." This reasoning completely ignored the difference between what God alone chooses to do and what theologians such as Barth and Bonhoeffer would say about what should be expected of believer decisions or actions that are presumably "under God." "Rahab" type logic suggests bargaining with—if not tempting—God, as implied in, "If you are God, then . . . " (Exodus, 17:7; Deuteronomy 6:16; Matthew 4:7).

After President Trump was in office a year, many newspapers were still publishing letters by Trump supporters arguing, "We care only what he has done since taking office," with rebuttals citing many of the not–so–Christian things he had done. Others stated, "Trump speaks and acts for us." Critics asked if statements such as "James Comey is a slime–ball" were Trump speaking "Christian" for them. Some noted that when Christian Trump supporters voted, they were likely Republicans first and Christians second. Other writers speculated that these Christians appeared to trade in many Christian values for a single–issue anti-abortion stance that came packaged with such things as hawkish foreign policy, easy gun access, anti-environmentalism, anti–immigration, and Ayn Rand unfettered capitalism. These opinions fit with what I called "smokescreen biblical morality," in which a strong, single–issue moral emphasis serves to obscure the lack of moral reasoning in many other moral issues. (A-10)

Early in the second year of the Trump presidency Christian engagement with politics still made local and national newspaper editorial pages. This news seemed mostly over the split between evangelicals who voted for Trump and the rest of American Christianity. Some newspaper letter-writers described the differences in the two sides as follows: Evangelicals believe you can be a good person but if you don't have a right belief that includes a proper stand on homosexuality and abortion you will be lost to God. Progressives think that living a life committed to compassion, justice, and peacemaking shows the authenticity of one's belief. One author concluded that these differences help explain why evangelicals continue to support Trump and progressives continue shaking their heads in disbelief.

These above comments support a theory that Trump may reflect a moral turn in US society more than a new moral challenge to it. A follow-up question is whether or not this reality is also a reflection on all Christian churches in the US, and whether some self-examination is in order regarding the effectiveness of its message.

The Fear Factor

The overriding question addressed in two editorials in the June 2018 issue of *The Christian Century* was: "Why would conservative evangelicals embrace someone whose life is so at odds with Christian values, especially when there were many other Republican candidates who had more solid credentials both as evangelists and conservatives?"[3] This question was described as something that bothered many Christians.

One answer to this loyalty question that seemed to supersede all others was that for evangelicals, there was an overriding sense of fear. Candidate Trump trumpeted this fear with supporting reasons that included Muslim immigrants, Mexican criminals, and foreign competition. The world was cheating Americans. These were real fears of Donald Trump and they meshed nicely with those of evangelicals (see pages 107–8). He agreed with them that what was needed was a strongman, and he was the best fit for the job.

President Trump's agenda for Christianity includes an effort to again say "Merry Christmas," a tradition allegedly threatened by political correctness promulgated by liberal media that he will stand up to. The problem is that although God may use either strong or weak persons to work his will, he does not accept boastful offers: "God chose what is weak in the world to shame the strong." (I Corinthians 1:27)

An article titled "The Fear Sweepstakes" in the same issue of *The Christian Century* detailed how Trump became the Republican strongman who could right the ship. At a critical point in the primary campaign Senators Cruz and Rubio seemed to have more authentic piety and faith. But Trump was appealing to a different type of evangelical: the entrepreneurial, "health and wealth," prosperity types. Desperate times allegedly require tough choices. One prominent evangelical pastor was quoted as saying, "When I'm looking for a leader . . . I want the meanest, toughest person possible to be president. "Trump was no novice when it came to fearmongering." Part of his genius was recognizing the fear in that sector of American Christianity and adding his own to solidify evangelical support and loyalty despite his anti–biblical reputation. For them, "Make America great again" meant to regain their stature and hopes for more. But when a prominent church leader, without special justification, seeks "meanest and toughest" persons as a coercive means to desired ends, it is suspect of a deviant theology of glory. It also shows no regard for Jesus' many admonitions to "Fear not!" (see page 109).

One type of fear that President Trump does not display is a reverential fear of God as outlined in Chapter 5. His moral failings with a regular disregard for the truth belie most tenets of biblical Christianity. An additional risk of such a "protector of Christianity" ideology is that the method and

3. Heim, "Public Witness and How it is Compromised," 7.

message of such political engagement may obscure more than point to the witness of Jesus in the world.[4]

Zero Tolerance

Consistent with the Trump fear theme, the Trump administration incorporated double-dose fear in implementing the zero tolerance project against asylum seekers with children by (a) exploiting the fear of his supporters and (b) generating fear of child separation from parents to deter asylum seekers.

In announcing the zero-tolerance immigration policy in Spring of 2018, Attorney General Jeff Sessions, Trump Chief of Staff John Kelly, and Senior Political Advisor Stephan Miller all noted that the policy was intended to deter immigrants. Attorney General Sessions quoted Romans 13:1 to justify the separation of children from their parents: "Let every person be subject to the governing authorities." Sessions failed to note, however, that the same Romans passage was cited by many in Germany as reasons to obey Hitler, and by Americans to justify US slavery.

Paul's statement in Romans 13 has usually been regarded as valid only when a law in question complies with God's laws: "We must obey God rather than men." (Acts 5:29) As noted in chapter 3 (p. 85), in his *Ethics*, Dietrich Bonhoeffer said that "The Christian's duty to the government is binding on him until the government directly compels him to offend against the divine Commandment." Rosa Parks broke the law when she refused to move to the back of a bus. Jesus broke a law when he healed on the Sabbath. Sessions is Methodist and over 600 of his church's clergy signed a letter opposing his decision. Other church leaders also voiced their objections. This public rebuke of zero tolerance policy by Christian leaders was about the only moral bright spot early in this cruel affair.

It is difficult to make all government policies optimally godly or biblical, but attempts can and usually have been made to have some parts of US policy reflect sound biblical principles. The Declaration of Independence declares that all persons are created equal and endowed by a Creator with certain inalienable equal rights. Such human rights are enumerated in the U.S Constitution and are upheld by following due process consistent with justice themes of the Bible.

4. Heim, "Public Witness and How it is Compromised," 7.

It became obvious that a policy to deter asylum seekers required selection of an action that would be significantly dreadful in comparison to how previous administrations had dealt with children. Dreadful cruelty was accomplished by essentially changing the charge for first time illegal entry for asylum requests from a misdemeanor to a felony. Felony or criminal status required prison detention and separation from children. As if this were not cruel enough, lack of immediate or complete knowledge of where children were located in relationship to their parents, barring the press from detention sites and moving children in the middle of the night caused one former immigration official to label the policy initiative "malevolent incompetence."

Jesus said, "Whoever receives one such child in my name receives me . . . If anyone of you put a stumbling block before one of these little ones who believe in me, it would be better if a great millstone were put around your neck and you were thrown into the sea." (Matthew 18:1–7; Mark 9:37, 42 NRSV) Jesus also said, "Let the little children to come unto me . . . " (Matthew 19:14), and "I was a stranger and you did not welcome me . . . depart from me." (Matthew 25:41)

Deliberate harm of children is one of the most egregious breaches of biblical morality. One suggested reason in addition to their intrinsic worth is that children are more innocent than adults, meaning they are more teachable since their ego has not yet petrified some selfish ideology: "Unless you turn and become like children, you will never enter the kingdom of God." (Matthew 18:3) Attempts at biblical justification make actions that are cruel to children that much worse.

Many things in President Trump's remote and recent history might be judged as questionably biblical or anti-Christian. But the shrewdly calculated plan to cruelly separate children from their parents as a means of deterring asylum seekers without serious planning for accommodating and reuniting parents with their children exposes the nature of this morality more than most Trump actions. In relationship to my selected biblical themes, the following judgments about the Trump administration zero tolerance policy are suggested:

- The policy reflects a habit of mostly interpreting the Bible by secular events rather than vice versa.

- The policy displaces an authentic theology of the cross with a corrupted theology of glory.

- The policy dismisses the relevance of the Old Testament prophets.

- The policy honors Ayn Rand's virtue of selfishness ideology over biblical holistic stewardship.

- The policy ignores the biblical concept of two kingdoms.

- The policy does not demonstrate a reverential fear of God.

- The policy serves to undermine more than protect American Christianity.

- The policy is driven largely by fear and ethnic whiteness rather than bold affirmation that "All men are created equal and endowed by their Creator with certain inalienable rights."

Some conservative stance may argue that these defects are overruled by any anti-abortion ideology. But this would ignore that fact all the women who brought their children to the US border seeking asylum had chosen not to abort those children.

With the new zero tolerance border policy, the picture emerged of the richest and most powerful nation on earth inflicting parent–separation cruel punishment on innocent vulnerable children as pawns in a scheme to discourage future refugees from seeking US asylum as authorized by international and US law. In so far as this is linked with President Trump's promise to defend American Christianity, by biblical standards his policy may undermine more than protect Christianity. This linkage of government power in this manner may fit the criteria of a theology of the cross humanly changed into a theology of glory (pages 17–18).

Societal Reasons to be Concerned

It is only to state the obvious that we Americans all should have community and not only individual reasons to be morally concerned about the health of our country. But in this context, it seems fitting to expand on one of the societal warnings cited in an earlier chapter from John Bright:

> But will we then commit the fatal error? Will we, like ancient Israel, imagine that our destiny under God and God's purposes in history are to be realized in terms of the society we have built? The temptation to do so is subtle. . .Surely, we think, God will protect us and give us the victory!

To this hope, Amos speaks a resounding No! Let us understand his words clearly: God does not in that sense have a favored people. No earthly society is established by God, guaranteed by God, and identified with his purposes. Nor does any earthly order, however good, have the means of setting up God's order in terms of its own ends. On the contrary, all societies are under the judgment of God's order, and those that have been favored with the light doubly so!

Indeed, before we can ever hope of having a righteous society established by God, we must, like Israel, learn that our order is not God's but must conform to it or perish. Wherever men have known of righteousness can only speak of their right to crowd for what they can get; wherever men who have known of Christian brotherhood behave as if they believed in favored races; wherever men who have heard a higher calling grow soft in the enjoyment of the ease that money can buy—there is society under judgment. And the judgment is history. Nor will it greatly matter to those who have to face it whether the barbaric tool of that judgment is Assyria or Russia.[5]

It also seems appropriate to add this warning from Isaiah:

"Ah, Assyria, the rod of my anger, the staff of my fury! Against a godless nation I send him, and against the people of my wrath send him. . ." (Isaiah 10:5). If God could use such a brutal power as Assyria to punish Israel for its waywardness, should it be surprising that a highly respected theologian could suggest that Russia or almost any country could become an instrument of God's judgment toward the US? In formulating an answer to this question, the following bulleted summary of relevant value changes under Trumpism compared to the best of American history might be considered:

- Falsehood increased over truth

- Selfishness increased over generosity

- Whiteness increased over diversity

- Fear increased over moral courage

These factors are important "means" toward Trumpism's "ends" to "Make America Great Again." Alternative visions of both means and ends could be formulated in both scientific and unscientific spheres of reality.

5. Bright, *The Kingdom of God*, 68–69. *Bibliography*

Trumpism appears to be deficient in both disciplines, and needs to be challenged by realistic alternatives. One alternative framework serves as an example.

Toward an Unscientific Conclusion

The title of one of Soren Kierkegaard's major books is *Concluding Unscientific Postscript*. As a scientist interested in Bible–News and Bible–science issues, for many years I have been curious about what theologians mean by "unscientific." By unscientific, Kierkegaard refers to a way of thinking that is subjective as distinct from objective in serious thinking about issues that make up important parts of human existence. Science is probably the discipline most closely identified with objective thinking because in its field of establishing truth in the natural or "material" world, science can usually use verification methods that render subjective human opinion theoretically irrelevant to the process. Science per se is often considered ethically neutral.

Objectivity regarding truth in its usual meaning of "unbiased" has many appropriate applications outside of science, such as in rendering non-prejudicial legal judgments. Subjective thinking often implies self–serving bias. Therefore, most people aware of such meanings try to be intellectually objective persons (Note that Ayn Rand labeled her own philosophy Objectivism). However, in Kierkegaard's view a problem exists in that "The majority of persons are subjective toward themselves and objective towards all others, terribly objective sometimes — but the real task in fact is to be objective towards ourselves and subjective toward all others."[6] In other words, we by nature easily love ourselves but have considerable difficulty loving others. Objectivity in living out "You shall love your neighbor as yourself," is not easy. G.K. Chesterton seemed to be thinking along these lines when he said, "The Christian ideal has not been tried and found wanting. It has been found difficult; and left untried."

Furthermore, science per se may be ethically neutral, but its use or misuse of it by human beings is not. The subjective realm of thinking is where knowledge of right vs. wrong, truth vs. falsehood, good vs. evil, and generosity vs. greed operate. This spiritual realm of existence is terribly important, because science or objective thinking alone cannot fundamentally control such realities. An extreme example is useful.

6. Kierkegaard, *Works of Love,* 13, *Bibliography*

There is general agreement that the misuse of medical science in the killing camps of the Holocaust did not reside in any "objective" inherent corruption in science per se. Rather, the major flaw in this horror resided in the subjective moral–spiritual context in which science was applied. Testimony from the Nuremberg trials established that many physicians were corrupted by Nazi ideology to the point that they believed that what they were doing was right: "They believed that thy had acted ethically in setting out to sterilize and destroy Jews, Gypsies, homosexuals and others perceived as threats to the racial health of the German nation."[7] In that circumstance, both traditional medical ethics and cultural Christianity had failed. Kierkegaard's arguments for the very important role of the subjective– unscientific realm of existence proved to be true. Karl Barth's Bible and Newspaper juxtaposition of two kingdoms may also be considered a juxtaposition of what Kierkegaard considers the unscientific with the scientific. This makes Trumpism seem more in line with with Ayn Rand's Objectivism than with the Bible.

Unscientific route to "Make America Great Again."

Some final thoughts relate to President Trump's slogan, "Make America Great Again." What eras or criteria the "again" in "Make America Great Again" refers to are murky, except for some allusions to "winning again." But this "winning" seems to aim to make others losers rather than achieving the better "win–win" outcomes. I would suggest that the "spirit of truth" type of patriotism exhibited from 1945 to 1950 by President Harry Truman in his relationship to his Secretary of State, former General George C. Marshall could serve as a good model to replicate in any attempt to restore greatness. Both Truman and Marshall knew that the severe "win–lose" reparations placed on Germany after WW–I had a lot to do with the genesis of WW–II. These men did not want that to happen again. Marshall had been a young officer in the US Army during WW–I and he knew that history well.

In a 1947 Harvard University commencement speech Marshall first unveiled what became known as the Marshall plan:

> It is logical that the United States should do whatever it is able to do to assist in the return of normal economic health without which there will be no economic stability and also no peace. Our policy is directed not against any country or doctrine but against

7. Caplan, *When Medicine Went Mad*, v (Preface, also p.59). *Bibliography*

hunger, poverty, desperation an and chaos . . . An essential part of any successful action on the part of the United States is an under-standing on the part of the people of America of the character of the problem and the remedies to be applied. Political passion and prejudice should have no part.[8]

President Truman had already articulated the "Truman Doctrine" that helped Greece and Turkey fend off Communist threats, and he dem-onstrated strong leadership in getting the Marshall Plan approved with Republicans in the majority of both houses of Congress. The plan was passed in the spring of 1948, which prepared the ground for the founding of NATO in 1949. Securing these European allies was a big part of making America as secure and powerful as she was for the next sixty–five years. The Marshall plan was "win–win" diplomacy of the more biblical type com-pared to "win–lose" philosophies. President Trump's alternative approach may have put this coalition in jeopardy.

Some quotations from Marshall and Truman provide some relevant insight. When asked about his political preferences, Marshall often re-sponded: "My father was a Democrat and my mother was a Republican, but I'm an Episcopalian."

President Truman was once quoted, possibly with the Marshall plan in mind, "It is amazing what you can accomplish if you do not care who gets the credit." Another Truman quip is, "I never gave them hell. I just told the truth and they thought it was hell." Would that we had more citizens with a commitment to truth and statesmanship like that which Truman and Marshall exhibited. Then perhaps we could feel good about America again.

8. "Marshall Plan Speech." *Bibliography*

List of Opinion Titles Classified by Subject

I. Biblical

A. Biblical Interpretation

1. Myths about Myths (7/13)
2. Faith vs. Knowing (9/15)
3. God Owns Everything (1/11)
4. Noah on Unjustified Violence (11/15)
5. Isaiah for Today (8/12)
6. Atheism and Christmas (12/10)
7. The Bible: Unifying or Divisive? (5/12)
8. A Christian Partisan Theological Divide (2/12)
9. Quoting the Bible (6/10)
10. Biblical Morality (10/16)
11. An election loser? (2/17)
12. Religious Right vs. Religious Left (7/17)
13. In Defense of Progressive Christians (7/17)
14. Back to the Bible (10/17)

II. Science

B. Health Care

1. Heal the Sick (2/16)

2. Moral Health Diagnostics (11/13).
3. Health Care Partisanship (3/15).
4. Specialists vs. Basic Care # (10/09)
5. Obamacare is a First Step (7/12)
6. A Loophole in the ACA (3/13)
7. Health Care Debt (2/10)
8. Risking Bankruptcy from Health Care (2/12)
9. Reducing Health Care Costs (6/12)
10. Misrepresenting the ACA. (10/13)
11. Murderous Obamacare? (11/13).
12. Trashing Obamacare (11/14)
13. Improving the Best Health Care (5/12)
14. Badmouthing Other Health Systems (9/09)
15. Greed Vs. The Healthy Common Good (1/10)
16. The Cemetery is Closed (10/13)
17. Improving Minnesota's Health (4/16)
18. A Health Care Conversation with Rep. Heintzenman (5/16)
19. Repealing Obamacare (3/17)
20. Misrepresenting Governor Dayton (on health care) (3/17)
21. Market Forces do not Easily Fit Health Care # (3/17)
22. Biblical Health Care (6/17)

C. Homosexuality

1. Marriage Amending in Minnesota (10/12)
2. Ethics from the Valley ** (5/94).
3. Oppose Sexual Promiscuity # (3/95)
4. ELCA Members Were Not Duped (9/09)
5. ELCA has not "Left God." (1/10)
6. ELCA Leaders did not Fail (1/10)
7. Practicing Marriage (11/13).
8. Homosexual Parenting (5/11)
9. Biblical Political Correctness (8/16)
10. Ethics of Contraception (8/12)
11. Contraceptives for Health # (? /15)

D. Ecology, Global Warming

1. Till It and Keep It (6/14).
2. The Crime of Galileo (7/15)
3. Galileo Had It Right (8/15)
4. More on Galileo (9/15)
5. God's Global Warnings (10/15)
6. Lying About Climate (8/16)
7. Job and Hurricanes (9/17)

E. Gun Violence

1. Guns Are a Public Health Problem (12/12)
2. School Prayer and Gun Control? # (2/94)
3. Guns With and Without Bibles (1/13)
4. Guns and Human Nature (4/13)
5. Gun Violence Because God Left Out (12/12)
6. Comparative Gun Homicide Rates 8/14)
7. God, Guns, and Violence (6/14)
8. NRA Culpability (11/14)
9. Underlying Gun Debate (4/13)
10. Ferguson Facts (9/14)
11. Second Amendment Ambiguities (12/13)
12. Guns and Corvettes (1/13)
13. Guns vs. Health Care (9/14)
14. The Bell Tolls Again (2/18)

F. War, Torture, and Terrorism

1. Guns and War for Jesus' Sake (10/15.)
2. Joining the Religious Battle Has Consequences # (7/15)
3. Anti-Muslim Madness (9/16)
4. Godly Patriotism and Torture (12/14)
5. More on God and Torture (12/14)
6. Religion Kills - So Can Sarcasm (1/15)

7. Divisive American Meltdown (5/13)
8. Deceptive Questions ((9/16)

G. Refugees

1. Moral Man and Immoral Society (12/15
2. Acting on our Moral Standards (7/14)
3. New Pathways Homeless Advocacy (1/15).
4. Compassion Up Close (3/17)
5. Trump's Muslim Ban (5/17)
6. Anti-DACA Family Values (1/18)
7. Lost children (5/18)

III. Political, Economic, Foreign Policy

H. Political

1. Positive Partisanship (1/14)
2. Biblical Justice (8/11)
3. What is Jury Justice? (11/13).
4. Deadly Politics (10/13)
5. Obama's Executive Orders (10/12)
6. Where is the Lie? (5/12)
7. Should Eric Holder Resign? (6/13)
8. Nolan's Non-Betrayal (10/13).
9. Words: Handle with Care (2/15).
10. Outstate vs. Metro (8/17)
11. A Deafening Silence (8/17)

I. Economics

1. Biblical Economics (12/13).
2. Ideology Vs. Pragmatism (6/12).
3. The "Cliff:" Fiscal or Integrity? (1/13).

4. Our Current Reality (5/11)
5. House Candidate's Stance on Wealth (11/13).
6. Flawed Criticism of Nolan (10/14).
7. Tax Return Transparency (5/17)
8. Shameless Greed (12/17)

J. Foreign Policy

1. The Syrian Dilemma (9/13)
2. Iran Nuclear Treaty Risks (2/15)
3. God's Foreign Policy? (3/12)

Parentheses designate month and year of publication

Designates publications in the Minneapolis *Star Tribune* (**= *Metro Lutheran*)

Because only half of the 106 opinions are referenced for Bible–news commentary, the title list gives an added perspective on the variety and emphasis of the subject matter. The publication dates on some opinions are approximate because, while I tried to be methodical in my recordkeeping there are gaps, especially in the earlier years. I have newsprint copies of most opinions but not all clippings included publication dates, and computer file dates differ from publication dates. Neither the total number nor the dates of publication are essential to the themes of the book (see page 11).

Appendix B

Twenty–Five Original Opinions Selected from Each Subject Category

NOTE: (BD) INDICATES BRAINERD Dispatch; (ST) indicates Minneapolis Star Tribune

A. Biblical

A–3 God Owns Everything

I agree with the writer who suggested that it is false to claim the private business sector can flourish without good government and regulations. But to say that God creates all wealth falls short of the Bible's proclamation that that God created and therefore owns everything. This makes all of us temporary stewards with only two options: trying to be God's good stewards, or something less. There will be an accounting. In Jesus' words, "It will be like a man going on a journey, who called his servants and entrusted his property to them. . ."

God created the kingdom of David and its wealth. He also was the "invisible hand" that destroyed their wealth by using adjacent nations (Assyria, Babylon, and Persia) as his temporary "servants" to end the kingdom(s). This was because of backtracking on a covenant to love neighbors as one's self. Wealth had magnified a false sense of ownership that was at odds with living as God's stewards. Most Americans claim to believe in God, but it seems doubtful that most of us believe that this biblical view of history is real or relevant.

It takes no great insight to have a disturbing sense that our society is shot through with failures in being good stewards of the blessings bequeathed to us. We should at least ask ourselves if we, like ancient Israel, mistakenly think our affluence has been a sign of our godliness, when in reality it may have turned more of us to thinking it is OK to act like greedy owners.

If we wish to preserve our nation, it might help to return to the biblical concept of being God's stewards, and reject secular doctrines of captains of our fates, masters of our souls, and self-made owners. Otherwise, God may make us face our own "Babylonian captivity."

BD–1/14/2011

A–12 Religious Eight vs. Religious Left

In his recent Dispatch opinion, "The religious left's Second Coming," Cal Thomas asserts that, "Every sermon dedicated to politics is time taken from a pastor's main calling, which is to preach a message that will fit people for Heaven." Many would disagree.

Karl Barth, one of the greatest theologians of the last century once counseled, "Christians should figuratively carry a Bible in one hand and a newspaper in the other, always taking care to interpret the news by the Bible—not vice versa."

Martyred German pastor-theologian Dietrich Bonhoeffer was a good friend of Barth. In his "Ethics," written during the war, Bonhoeffer asks this poignant question: "Has the Church merely to gather up those whom the wheel has crushed or has she to prevent the wheel from crushing them?" After the War, Barth noted that the Church in Germany had seriously failed in its duty to resist Hitler—it failed to be responsibly political.

Thomas fails to relate his moral-political theology to two of the foundational provisions of the First Amendment to the US Constitution: free exercise of religion, and freedom of speech and the press. These provisions could give both the press and churches a loyal-opposition, watchdog relationship to governments in order to help insure their integrity.

The press has been pretty much able to maintain this watchdog function. Unlike Pope Francis, however, congregations have mostly abandoned such dialogue. Except, that is, for the Thomas/religious right's priority of three sexuality issues. Heaven and certain sexual purities seem to go together. Germany's fatal flaw was not primarily sexual, although Hitler imprisoned and killed many thousands of homosexual persons.

To abandon health care for millions of the born for the sake of the unborn and rich does not seem to qualify as a wholistic morality.

BD–7/1/17

B. Health Care

1. Heal the Sick

In his book, "The Healing of America," T. R. Reid, states that, "Unlike the other (20) developed countries of the world . . . we have never decided to make the fundamental moral decision to provide medical care for everybody who needs it." Since the most popular book for moral guidance in America is the Bible, it seems a moral thing to find relationships to American health care issues.

The four gospels have over forty references to Jesus' different acts of healing or admonitions for his followers to do the same. For example: "And preach as you go, saying, 'the kingdom of heaven is at hand. Heal the sick. . .'" (Matt. 10:7). In Matt. 25 Jesus is asked, "When did we see you sick and not come. . .?" A reasonable interpretation is that for Jesus, preaching the one without advocating good care for all may not cut it.

In this context, the fundamental question for all citizens whose money proclaims "In God We Trust" should be, "Do you share a moral vision that every U.S. citizen should have good access to affordable health care?" If the answer is "yes," the next question should be, "Is it good or bad that in the last five years the number of uninsured Americans has dropped from forty-five to thirty-five million?"

The instrument that changed this number is, of course, Obamacare. But many health care deficiencies continue. In coverage, cost, and outcomes, the US is not yet competitive with the most developed world. These countries insure essentially everyone at two-thirds or less our per capita cost. Their secret is something called single payer. A guy named Bernie Sanders is marketing it. If he can't succeed, Minnesota should have an opportunity in 2017 to have its own state plan like Romney gave Massachusetts. Stay tuned.

BD—2/4/16

B-5. Obamacare is a First Step

Since the recent Supreme Court decision on Obamacare Dispatch letters have warned of doomsday outcomes. These are old saws.

In 1964, I was in the first years of post-medical school graduate trained aimed at going into general practice in rural Minnesota. But Medicare legislation was about to pass with ominous warnings, including non-specialty physicians working only in government offices. I switched to internal medicine and cardiology. False fear mongering changed my career plans.

In 1969, my mother-in-law died of colon cancer at age 58 after being told she would no longer be covered for any "tumerous" condition." This would not happen in Canada or under Obamacare. In contrast, my own mother had her life extended seven years by renaldialysis, which was covered by Medicare.

Most of the early physician-opposition to Medicare vanished because it vastly improved the economics of health care for seniors. The Reagan administration passed a bill requiring providers to care for persons who receive care without ability to pay for it. In 1993, the Clinton single-payer plan was killed with arguments proposing a mandate program. Romney later passed a mandate program in Massachusetts, achieving 98% coverage.

The main health question is not about taxes or socialism. It is whether our government's constitutional responsibility to "provide for the general welfare" includes health care for all citizens. Or, should we remain ranked low in the industrialized world on this moral-quality/economic quotient?

In the past 35 years the market-force only theory for health has nowhere competitively approached this universality goal. The Tea party seems opposed to universal care. The court left the door open for a better system of freedom through this common good. Obamcare is a first step.

BD-7/8/12)

B—21 Free Market Health Care

Rep. Jason Lewis' defense of the GOP health plan in the March 18 Star Tribune outlines the first of three steps that promises to give "universal access to affordable health care." I found no convincing numbers in his "replace" argument, only ideological theory to "restore health care markets" and "increase health insurance choices. "Restore" suggests bringing something old back rather than attempting something new. The historical context is that total annual U.S. health care costs rose in almost a straight line from 5 percent of GDP in 1960 to almost 18 percent in 2010.

Rep. Lewis is obviously adopting and defending Rep. Paul Ryan's Ayn Rand-based unfettered capitalism theory applied to health care delivery. Such free market choice competition theories of cost control for medical care were credibly challenged by Stanford Nobel laureate economist Kenneth Arrow back in 1963. Arrow's analysis was in turn cited by Dr. Arnold Relman, the highly respected former editor of *The New England Journal of Medicine* in his health reform book, "A Second Opinion," published in 2007.

Arrow's thesis is: "The medical care system is set apart from other markets by some unique characteristics." These characteristics included:

1. Patient demand for services is for conditions that at unpredictable times rise to an existential threat from life-threatening illness or injury. This tilts buyer priority concerns away from costs toward quality;

2. Buyer demand for services does not simply respond to the desires of buyers, but is primarily determined by the professional judgment of physicians about the medical needs of their patients;

3. There are significant limitations on the entry of providers into the market resulting from the high costs and exacting standards of professional education;

4. There is a relative insensitivity to costs and a near absence of price competition (here referring to competition among providers, not insurers);

5. There is significant buyer market uncertainty because of the great asymmetry of knowledge between provider and buyer for a particular service, and the consequences of a course of action.

Arrow concluded that because of the way all these factors conspire, patients cannot independently decide what services they want in the same way consumers decide in the usual market when shopping for what they want at the price they want to pay. Because a higher level of trust is required in medical care than in most venues, society must rely on nonmarket mechanisms such as educational standards and state licensure, rather than on the discipline of the market and the choices of informed buyers.

The fundamental economic reality in the U.S. is that health care spending has risen faster than the gross domestic product at the same time wealth disparity among buyers has increased. If everyone is to receive care and these divergent trajectories continue, the affluent will have to pay more for those who can't afford it. By comparison in the same recent time frame, most of the other twenty most advanced world democracies have done much better at keeping health care costs in line with their GDPs. All of their citizens are guaranteed affordable care at 50—70 percent per capita cost of that in the U.S. with generally better outcomes. Most of these countries do this with some variation of single payer with private providers similar to Medicare. These facts and many others support Arrow's theory more than they undermine it.

Furthermore, most Republicans refer more to competition among insurance companies rather than among providers without giving evidence supporting the theory that competition among insurers inhibits costs and prices of providers.

The Ryan- GOP free market premise of free market capitalism to control costs is weak in both theory and supporting evidence. Republicans are in danger of betting on a false market premise that could make their formulations into more of a disaster. A safer bet against serious failure that could also expand the Republican base would be to fix Obamacare, or go straight to Medicare for all.

(ST–3/21/17)

C. Homosexuality

C–4 ELCA Members Were Not Duped

The letter writer who castigates local ELCA church members for not condemning the recent assembly actions seems uninformed. He thinks ELCA members and their assembly representatives (60% laity) are gullible and sadly misled by church leaders.

The writer apparently doesn't know that the ELCA discussions that led to this vote started 20 years ago, or that the resolutions that mandated an extensive study and discussions before this vote were passed in 2001. He has not likely seen how the study materials outline both traditional and nontraditional biblical interpretations and explain how they can be used to oppose or encourage policy changes. Nor has he seen how this study was set in the larger context of law and gospel theology. It is doubtful that he has been to congregational or synod meetings where gays, lesbians, parents, and friend of homosexual persons—individuals who have tried reparation therapy, etc., have all sat together with each other in respectful conversation with those who oppose change in policies.

All these opportunities have been open to any who claim to "love the sinner," as he does.

Like many other church bodies, the ELCA is divided on this issue, but not because its members were suddenly duped by some leasers. His judgmental attitude is a good example of what has turned many Christians to a fuller biblical understanding of God's love for all persons.

(BD–9/20/09)

C–7 Practicing Marriage

Since the passage of the Minnesota law authorizing same-sex marriage there has been a steady stream of letters from Dispatch readers opposed to it. I have, not, however, seen any letters that noted the important role of the opposition in facilitating the new law.

A year ago, Minnesota had a law prohibiting marriage of lesbian or gay couples.

Because this was not secure enough for many opposed to same sex marriage, a vote was put on the ballot to put this law into the state constitution. Some analysis has indicated that recently, the more open the debate there is on homosexual rights, the greater is the net move of opinion in favor of more equality. In addition, some of the anti-gay rhetoric is counterproductive. The opposition ignores these factors.

A trip-wire to those opposed to homosexual rights has been their misrepresentations of the consensus bio-medical-psychological science of homosexuality. Consensus here means over 97 percent of related professionals.Ever since the 1973 American Psychiatric Association (APA) actions, there has been a small minority of scientists who opposed this decision with their own literature and lobby groups.

The talking-point misrepresentations of the peer-reviewed scientific literature used by traditionalists have been turned back against the opposition as evidence of low integrity argumentation. Many of these false claims have been printed in recent Dispatch letters. These were on subjects such as homosexuality as a choice, adoption, and the causes of promiscuity and illness.

Marriage needs to be practiced more than it needs to be poorly defended verbally.

The APA stance has been primarily against discrimination, and even the 20 year ELCA deliberations produced only recommendations for same-sex partner blessings, not marriage. It was partly the flawed negativism of the anti-gay stance that gave lesbians and gays a bonus in Minnesota.

BD–11/1/13

D. Global Warming

D–1 Till It and Keep It

One of the early pages of the book of Genesis has the words, "The Lord God took the man and put him in the garden to till it and keep it." These words even preceded the "fall." "Keep it," means to preserve or conserve it. Thus, a foundational biblical intention for humankind is caring for nature.

From the beginning, trees and plants have been basic to what sustains animal and human life. Leaves and needles are nature's solar panels that transform the sun's energy into plant energy to fuel not only their own growth, but also to produce roots, seeds and fruit that sustains other life. The unique chemical involved is chlorophyll. Humans need it to survive more than chlorophyll needs humans to continue its life-sustaining function. In the Noah flood account, the sign that life could survive on land was an olive branch brought back by a sentinel dove. These stories may have profound clues not only about the beginning of human history, but also about its end.

Ancient thinking that presaged modern science identified four primary elements necessary for life besides sunlight: earth, air, water, and fire. These must be in a balance with one another in an optimal symbiotic relationship for human health. But our human actions suggest that we do not respect this rudimentary reality. Each gallon of gasoline comes from many tons of ancient plants that cannot be burned without emitting carbon dioxide. There is no likely way increasing consumption of this product of ancient plant life is renewably sustainable. But the political cries of many in our culture are still symbolized by "drill baby, drill."

The historical narrative that obscured human awareness of the "keep it" biblical mandate was the transformation that began in the 1700s with the industrial revolution, global capitalism, and increasing consumption. These factors smoldered up slowly until just after WW-II when all the great leaps in labor saving devices accelerated. The ingredient that made this science work with such deceptive efficiency was seemingly abundant sources of compact energy in the form of fossil fuels. The illusion was created that humans could bypass the rhythms of nature and create a new world on their own terms. But the foundations of this ideology are crumbling.

When plotted against the last 100 years of time, the consumption of energy and dozens of other products like paper, water, and fertilizer, all define a slow rise the first 50 years and then an increasingly rapid rise toward vertical (forming a "hockey stick" shape). \These graphs in turn replicate similar exponential rises of atmospheric carbon dioxide concentration, ozone depletion, rise in average earth surface temperature, species extinction, and many other factors. The striking correlation of all these changes has no precedent. We are therefore like a ship sailing in uncharted waters. The apostle Paul's words, "The whole creation groans in travail" are more evident for earth today than even a generation ago.

The danger is not only from extractions deep in the earth, but also from the many dangerous substances dispersed on its surface. The song of meadowlarks has almost disappeared from our prairies, and honeybees are not pollinating like they used to - signals of much broader species extinction. Such outcomes have been linked to an earth-exploitation doctrine that asserts a wealth-disparity ignited desire for riches is the most effective stimulus for human creativity and societal prosperity. This shortsighted ideology runs counter to the biblical mandate to partner with nature in mutual health-preserving enterprises. No human can create a blade of grass. Therefore at least those who judge the Bible to be the best revelation of divine and moral reality should look back to the biblical mandate "to till and to keep it."

Journalist Thomas Friedman recently pointed out that the looming crisis would not necessarily be deletion of fossil fuels. The chief economist of the International Energy Agency has declared that "about 2/3 of all proven reserves of oil, gas, and coal will have to be left undeveloped if the world is to achieve the goal of limiting global warming to 2 degrees Celsius since the Industrial Revolution." Crossing that line is where scientific consensus estimates severe ecological disruptions will occur that may be unmanageable. Many nations are ahead of us on wind and solar power. The US led the world into this predicament and if we don't lead the way out, we will lose whatever moral high ground the rest of the world grants us.

One prominent theologian cites a psychological experience that could lead to ecological attitude change known as "the shock of recognition." This happened to Robert Oppenheimer, the civilian head of the Manhattan project, after he witnessed the explosion of the first atomic bomb. Quoting Vishnu in Hindu scripture he said he felt, "I am become death, the destroyer of worlds." Another example could be the point Noah's neighbors saw the rising floodwaters lift his boat off the ground. But obviously the only factor for such shock recognition does not have to be water. In any case, one can hope that by that time it is not too late.

It matters little whether the next major recognition of global ecological carelessness is conflict over energy scarcity, multiple climatic disasters, costly species extinctions, or some other revelatory occurrences from unseen hand of the Creator. Biblical setback events are portrayed partly as ways of preventing humans from completely extinguishing themselves. Sneering at all the warning signals against drill and spread ideologies are dangerous.

The challenging task of this and future generations is to learn to live within the means of the earth's ability to re-charge its resources, aided by wind and solar means. We need a reverse transition from the nature devastation age we are in, into mutually productive ways of preserving our "spaceship earth." If we don't, greedy power plays to control nature and society will risk increasing domestic and international violence. And future generations may label ours as one of the most selfish in history.

(BD-6/15/14)

D-3 Galileo Had It Right

When I first read the August 16 Dispatch letter challenging my comparison of Galileo's coerced recantation of the Copernican solar theory with the current global warming debate, I wondered if it might be a vain attempt at mocking sarcasm. He admonishes some common sense, while his formulation contains little historical, logical, or relevant scientific sense.

My critic makes the remarkable claim that "The Galileo heliocentric theory has no basis today." In reality, the "common sense" heliocentric theory is as factual today as it was in 1633. Heliocentric simply means "relating to the sun as a center" (Webster) compared to geocentric - relating to the earth as a center. The Galileo issue was about the spatial and motion relationships of our sun (star) and its planets. The letter attempts to shift the debate to the position of the earth "in the known universe." On this false premise regarding the Galileo event he concludes Galileo was wrong on "three strikes." But even the Catholic Church eventually admitted it was wrong and Galileo had it right.

My commonsense comparison of the Galileo event to the current global warming issue was clearly stated. I was simply comparing the dogmatic certainty of the stance against Galileo with the similar certainty of many current opponents of global warming. Subjective confidence has little relationship to factual truth. I made no inferences that the Galileo affair had any direct scientific fact relevance to either side in the global warming debate.

The writer's critique did not challenge my conclusion: "In our time, over 90% agreement by scientists most qualified to make judgments on a scientific question usually predicts that their answer will be established as fact." I stand with this majority of qualified, peer-reviewed, publishing scientists on the global warming issue.

(BD-8/28/15)

E. Gun Violence

E-2 How about Allowing School Prayer in Exchange for Gun Control?

The irony of the coincidence on the Star Tribune's editorial page Nov 29 should not go unnoticed. The staff editorial poignantly described one of thousands of domestic handgun-caused tragedies, and the Counterpoint by a local pastor blames lack prayer in the public schools for violence in homes (along with a host of other problems). The connection is more than coincidental. Those invoking the Constitution as the basis for public school prayer more often than not use the same claim against gun control.

If politics is the art of compromise, perhaps a generic prayer against violence could be allowed in return for more restriction of citizen ownership of handguns. Even without the National Rifle Association (NRA) this would be unlikely, however, because for much of the nation, faith is a "God helps those who help themselves" variety, with guns being not only a constitutional, but also a God-given right.

The pastor's position is that things went bad starting in 1963, when prayer in the public schools was outlawed. My recollection of the 60s is highlighted by the assassination of John and Robert Kennedy and Rev. Martin Luther King, and our "slippery slope" into Vietnam. The Vietnam affair interrupted two years of my career when I saw some of its gun-related bodily and psychic damage. Vietnam policy decisions were made by those who went to school in the "good old days" when prayer was allowed in schools and I see a more direct connection between our current violence epidemic and the '60s "Rambo" right to coerce than a lack of school prayer.

More recently guns again interrupted my career. I was required to serve as a juror on a robbery-murder case in which the "slippery slope" for the defendant began when he exercised his constitutional right to buy one gun a week so he could resell them at a profit on the streets. The gun dealer who sold him one gun a week for six months (under his constitutional and NRA-encouraged right) was legally immune, even though a gun he sold was used to murder a clerk in another gun shop. The murdered clerk was shot in the face from 6 feet away while holstering a handgun—so much for my confidence in handguns as deterrent or protection.

I do not begrudge my country the time I spent in the military or as a juror—they were minor inconveniences compared to the agonies of the handgun deaths described in the Star Tribune staff editorial. But like more people, I find

it increasingly difficult to remain silent about the insanity of the increasing violence and the role of handguns, the NRA and some religious groups in fueling the
epidemic.

As one who claims to be Christian, I must disagree with those Christians
who oppose gun control or remain silent about it and instead make school prayer
a scapegoat. I believe less faith in guns and a more demonstrable faith that would
limit handguns to law enforcers would be more authentic and better for society
than arming ourselves, while forcing our particular prayers on all of our neighbor's
children in public schools.

(ST–12/10/94)

E-3 Guns With and Without Bibles

The December 21 Brainerd Dispatch published a guest opinion titled, "Why Was
God AWOL at Newtown?" by Robert Ringer, a conservative columnist. The essay
is, therefore, an intriguing example of a conservative moral framework from which
to view the tragic use of weaponry in the Newtown grade school. The foundational
premise for this stance is, "Bad things happen. It's an inescapable reality of life,"
repeated immediately in a longer paraphrase.

Ringer then builds on this foundation by exploring the "age old spiritual and
philosophical question of, why does God allow evil and injustice to exist in the first
place?" In his formulation, understanding evil and its relationship to a possible
God are central to understanding the "vicissitudes of life," including Newtown.
Bringing in God makes the topic theological. A common oversimplified theological answer to the God and evil question is usually something like, "If God wanted
a world without evil, humans would all need to be robots with no free will. No
doubt the rest of creation would be better off if humans were all Chimpanzees, but
God apparently thought granting a measure of free will was worth it." Ringer didn't
mention free will.

One does not have to postulate a God in order to make the following moral
judgment about an event: "This should not have happened." Secular philosophers
would likely agree Newtown represents moral evil rather than a natural evil because it was a human act, not an earthquake or a chance illness.

But Ringer tries to dig deeper. Most of his position paper addresses questions about whether God exists or can be considered good. After superficially citing
multiple sources he hesitantly seems to come down on the Christian existence side
when he cites Reinhold Niebuhr's Serenity Prayer and concludes, "The challenge
. . . is to understand which things are within our control and which things are not."

Some nuances suggest a certain amount of "fatalism" that accommodates "things I (we) cannot change" in preventing another Newtown. In his book "Moral Man and Immoral Society," Niebuhr is a social activist when it comes to dealing with social evil.

In the end Ringer leaves us with no specific concrete proposals, strongly suggesting he favors the status quo in terms of any gun control. Some other characteristics of his exploration are worth noting. Ringer's essay includes the word God 23 times, the word evil seven times, and the word gun only once, but not in reference to their use in the killing. Remarkably, the Bible is never referenced nor the word used, even though the Bible uses the word evil over 600 times and the word God over 4500 times. Why does he ignore it? A reasonable conclusion is that the Bible presents significant difficulties for use it in an ethical analysis of gun-related evil. An example of a biblically based framework, starting with Niebuhr, can demonstrate reasons why Ringer avoids the Bible.

In at least several of his works, Niebuhr asserts that a central component that leads persons to commit evil acts is human anxiety. A major cause of anxiety is fear of violence, and this anxiety in turn predisposes to acts of violence. Frequently, an attempt to increase personal power is the preferred means to suppress this anxiety. Relational trust in someone can decrease anxiety, especially in children.

Jesus admonished, "Do not be anxious. . ." (Matt. 6:25). Faith and trust are synonyms. Jesus is believed to have been compassionate, righteous and innocent of the charges that led him to be violently put to death by the strongest nation of his time. Paradoxically, this historical violence against human innocence became transformed into a source of hope and comfort, including many of the millions pondering the Newtown massacre.

Twenty years ago a respected theologian, Marjorie Suchockie, building on the works of Niebuhr wrote a book titled, "The Fall to Violence." Her thesis is that the most universal aspect of Adam and Eve's fall is what immediately followed in the next chapter of Genesis: "Cain rose up against his brother and killed him." Suchokei's view is that anyone who acts destructively against the well-being of another person or any part of creation, replicates the "Original Sin" described in the Bible, whether or not the perpetrator believes the Bible or that sin is a rebellion against God.

Niebuhr died in 1971, and I don't know if he ever addressed the Second Amendment issue, although he did protest US military involvement in Viet Nam. Suchockie, however, connects guns as a means of obtaining a sense of power and security to decrease anxiety. After citing a gun event in her book she wrote, "Someone made the guns available to the children . . . Corporate greed for ever greater profits from gun sales results in an incredible proliferation of guns throughout American culture, all under the reasoning that if everyone has guns, everyone can protect the self from everyone else. Do not these other persons share in the (moral) guilt of the death? . . . The American obsession with guns and violence . . . is our attempt to delude ourselves into believing that we can control the firing of our weapons, that we can confine our violence through channeling it into an arena or ring, and that we can turn the power of our televisions off, and so control the violence that we safely allow into our lives. But anxiety mocks our control. Violence, not death, is at the root of our anxieties, and our attempts to channel violence simply increases its ceaseless flow."

I favor at least banning assault weapons. I would also like to see a biblically based credible essay that justifies personal ownership and use of such weapons.

(BD–12/28/12)

War, Torture, and Terrorism

F–1 Guns and War for Jesus' Sake

An October 7 letter alleges that President Obama downgrades our nation's "Christian religion" by urging more gun control and not responding in kind to Muslims' killing of Christians overseas. The author claims the US should take action "to stop the growth of Islam" because President Obama's inaction fulfills Jesus' prophecy that, "You will be hated by all nations for my name's sake."

The premise of the letter is that love for Jesus should be demonstrated by an "eye for an eye" retribution for violence directed at followers of Jesus. Failure to take such action is to hate Jesus. The biblical record of Jesus' life, death, ministry, and his own words shout otherwise. Jesus was rejected in his day because a Messiah was expected to bring freedom by violent means, which he failed to do. The Christian church was a minority persecuted by the state in the rapid growth of its first 300 years, but Christians never lifted a sword against Rome.

In contrast, US claims to be a Christian nation coupled with its violent interventions in Middle East Muslim countries is a hypocritical face the US has given its Christianity, not what authentic Christianity is. Torture and preemptive war with claims "God is on our side" helped fuel extremist hatred of the US and create ISIS. Jesus was hated because he spoke truth to power about justice, and he exposed moral hypocrisy by non-violent means. Martin Luther King is a good example of an authentic Christian witness.

In a sinful world, in-place violent deterrence measures become necessary. But it is more Christian to stand for "well regulated" private gun ownership and work hard diplomatically to avoid war than to push for the opposite. In contrast to the letter's allegations, President Obama has been following the more Jesus way.

(BD–10/23/15)

F–2 Joining the Battle has Consequences

The recent Counterpoint opinion on the religious nature of recent wars presents an interpretation of The Kingdom of God that is not very biblical. The writer proposes that American Christians should "join the battle" with our "mighty armed national brotherhoods" in "wielding a "sword of protection" for world-wide persecuted Christians. He asserts Christians have a "duty to defend that kingdom," so "Christian men formed police departments and national armies and navies." The creation of a coercive force is exactly what a majority in Jesus' society expected a messiah to do. But Jesus told Pilate, "My kingdom is not from this world. If it were, my followers would be fighting to prevent my arrest."

In the first 300 years of the rapid growth of the Christian church, it was a persecuted minority that did not take up the sword to defend his kingdom. Constantine's melding of church and state resulted in what Martin Luther called many subsequent perverted theologies of glory that displace a more biblical theology of the cross. The "join the battle" opinion provides an example.

This writer ignored the relevance of the US preemptive Iraq war, launched with many Christian platitudes. It displaced a Sunni dictator with an elected Shiite president that excluded Sunnis, some of which then became the core of ISIS and the Levant. The result is that Christians in the region are now much worse off than they with Saddam in power. We are a part of the problem and war promoters irrationally want more of the same as a solution. (ST–7/26/15)

F–4 Godly Patriotism and Torture.

A recent letter in the Dispatch concluded, "We need to return to God and Patriotism." The problem with this admonition is its ambiguity: "return" is to what time and specifics? What is the relationship between God and patriotism, if any? One person's patriotism is unpatriotic to another. Regardless, the important question is: "What is God's judgment about any patriotism?" The recent Senate committee report on torture provides an apt working example, and the differences between President Bush and President Obama are instructive.

Bush repeatedly asserted, "God is on our side" while he simultaneously authorized the "enhanced interrogation techniques" (EITs), defined legally as a torture crime by the UN and Geneva Conventions. On taking office, Obama immediately stopped the program. Obama claims to be Christian but he never asserted, "God is on our side (in this war)."

But if one were absolutely confident that God were on his side, shouldn't "In God We Trust" mean avoiding the dubiously effective practice of torture in any circumstance?

Dietrich Bonhoeffer was a German theologian martyred for his resistance to Hitler. In his *Ethics* he argues that the moral witness of Christians should not consist of one sphere for biblical religion (or church) separated from another sphere for the so-called secular world. This is because such a camouflaged division—implicitly present in Germany at the time—is a denial of God's reconciliation of the whole world. Rather, there should be one ethic, such that the church, family, business, labor, and government should all be regarded as within one sphere of morality. Christians should strive to live within this one moral sphere in all of life. God is over all and all are accountable to God.

The main point here is that simply juxtaposing God and patriotism in a paragraph doesn't constitute a stance that is credibly godly or patriotic. I consider my stance against torture as patriotic and Christian even as I differ in specifics from others also claiming to be patriotic and Christian. I subscribe to the view that whether Islamic, Judaic or Christian, a religious certainty that replaces faith can make war more barbaric and immoral rather than less so. We readily see this in others but not in ourselves.

The same "one sphere" Christian ethic should also apply to other debatable issues such as preemptive war, health care, gun rights, immigration policy, "unfettered capitalism" (Pope Francis), wealth disparity, environmental preservation, family values, and quality of civil discourse. Pursuant to this goal the use of the Bible can be manipulated into irrelevance.

Yale theologian Leander Keck has suggested that many Christians operate with a compartmentalized misuse of the Bible that resembles children who pick cherries they like out of the fruitcake they otherwise dislike. The whole Bible must be used, but one can at least start with Jesus' teachings about loving our neighbors and move to the unjust practices the prophets cited against Israel and Judah. Regarding torture, we should remember that Jesus was tortured and crucified under charges of treason. He also said, "I was in prison and you visited [cared for] me."

The biblical witness is that short-term immoral expediency can be deceiving because God's invisible finger in history may grind out deserving judgments slowly.

We may have witnessed this. The preemptive Iraq war lowered the moral ground from which President Obama had to stand against Russia's similar preemptive seizure of Crimea. The democracy we helped establish in Iraq replaced Iraq's minority Sunni government with a Shiite majority hostile to Sunnis. Disgruntled former Sunni generals and soldiers of Saddam's dismantled army later became the core of the ISIS movement that we now have to still fight. Similar long-tern consequences, including more capture and torture of US soldiers, citizens, could still follow from Cheney era torture actions.

So, would the Dispatch writer's "return" prefer going back to the Bush certainty of whose side God was on linked with a Cheney view of EITs? Or would he go back farther to 1988 when President Reagan signed on to the UN International Convention Against Torture (ratified in 1994) that codified water boarding as torture? Some specifics are required for a credible promotion of both God and patriotism.

BD–12/26/14)

F-6 'Religion kills'—So Does Sarcasm

Charles Krauthammer's Jan. 16 Dispatch commentary outlines his theory of the US war on terror since 9/11 in three worsening phases. In the most recent *Atlantic Monthly,* James Fallows would agree with the worsening part. But, quoting intelligence officials, he argues that although the U.S. tactically won all battles in the wars since 9/11, by strategic goals set at the start, we lost the wars. Al Qaida is alive and active, and it helped spawn ISIS.

The strategic failure was faulty analysis of the enemy, and the premise that successful military action alone can finish the job. Putting troops on the ground thousands of miles away where there is significant indigenous opposition is not conventional warfare or a winnable combination. Locking down five or more countries with 250,000 troops each for 10 years might not have been much better. Fallows thinks that it would have been better if the $trillion-plus spent had just been burned.

The Vietnam war, in which I served, has similarities to the post 9/11 Afghanistan and Iraq wars. A significant difference, however, is that the Al Qaida and ISIS wars have an added dimension of inter-religious hostility. This is a mix that needs to be taken seriously. On that count we need to be reminded that at the time of the Iraq invasion, a significant number of Christians including the Pope, Catholic bishops, the World Council of Churches and many protestant bishops and theologians opposed that invasion. One such voice was poignantly prophetic:

Christians—and especially Western Christians—who imagine that the epithet 'Religion Kills,' scrawled on a wall in NYC after 9–11, has no application to themselves and their religions are greatly deceived . . . It can in fact be argued (and is) that the current [2003] bellicosity of the militant forms of Islam represents a reaction of the Muslim world to its humiliation by the powerful technocratic West . . . which includes . . . the most avowedly Christian of all the nations of the world . . . There is a current protest of mainstream Christians in the U.S. and elsewhere against the evident desire of the governing authorities of America to launch a 'preventive' war in Iraq. They realize that violence alone can only beget more violence." (Douglas John Hall, "The Cross in Our Context," 2003).

The general indictment that "Religion kills" has not been refuted. But some concerned Christians had the problem pegged right from the start. Terrorists don't expect the West to collapse under their attacks. What they likely hope for is a violent response to help radicalize peace-loving Muslims, along with forcing a slow bleeding of the West. Thus the preemptive war in Iraq that killed over 100,000 Iraqis gave Al-Qaida exactly what it wanted.

Back in 2002–03 Krauthammer supported the weapons of mass destruction (WMD) theory justifying the Iraq invasion. He apparently doesn't see that war theory and war as relevant to his present war theory. He still is hawkish, both militarily and on the free-speech-sarcasm action that sparked the recent Paris attacks. Sarcasm looks like backup response to lost war mentality, but it also can radicalize Muslims. Like it or not, both "I am Charlie Hebdo" and Krauthammer sarcasm represent a Christian West expression of biblical faith.

The Bible has something to say about appropriate vs. inappropriate speech and actions: "Let your speech always be gracious;" "Be a model of sound speech;" "All things are lawful but not all things are beneficial;" "Repay no one evil for evil." "Blessed are the peacemakers," "Do good to those who hate you," "By their fruits you will know them." Such verses underlie Christian ethics. As such, why shouldn't terrorists consider mocking insults as rank hypocrisy or phony religion?

That question and controversial war theories aside, one might at least make the case that using disrespectful speech or writing that employs sarcasm and/or obnoxious insults ought to be avoided. This is especially the case when directed at a group that has been humiliated by the Christian West for centuries. If "winning" the moral argument is considered important rather than just military battles, the issue about good speech in free speech is relevant. This is a point conservative columnist David Brooks made in his recent New York Times opinion, "I am not Charlie Hebdo."

The other moral question also still stands: Does religion that appears callous to human rights make wars more likely and deadlier rather than less? If the answer is "yes," it should be accepted as valid only with the recognition of another claim: that within authentic Judaism, Islam, and Christianity there have for centuries been significant numbers that stand for anti-torture policies, just war principles, and respect for cultural differences.

I think Jesus abhors war. But when his followers are caught in it, I believe he prefers that they stand with the latter group.

(BD–1/23/15)

G. Refugees

G–1 Moral Man and Immoral Society

The world is facing one of the biggest refugee crises in history and the United States is very divided on the question of whether or not to accept refugees from Iraq and Syria. The US is also avowedly one of the most Christian nations on earth and therefore Christians face the question of whether or not this biblical faith has any relevance on what refugee policy should be. One of the most relevant American theologians on the relationship of faith to government and politics is Reinhold Niebuhr, especially his book, "Moral Man and Immoral Society."

Niebuhr observed that individual humans have great capacity to act with compassion for the wellbeing of others. However, when they organize into like-minded competitive groups, the group ego morality takes on a hypocrisy and self-ishness not characteristic of its individual members. The phenomenon is roughly proportional to the power relationships involved, so the risk to well–being is most pronounced in nation-states. This risk should be diligently guarded against - but it usually isn't.

Moral analysis of the migrant crisis should look at its cause. The immediate cause is ISIL (or ISIS). But the root cause is the preemptive invasion of Iraq that led to a new government that excluded the disgruntled and defeated Sunni military that formed the initial core of ISIL. The war killed over 150,000 Iraqis, over half of them non-combatants. A sense of injustice committed against Iraq in the name of Christian ideals created a revenge mentality linked to perverted Islamic doctrine. ISIL's mission is to exact justice on these terms.

In applying the above Niebuhr thesis to the Iraq war, it can be argued that the ethical justification of the Iraq invasion was an expedient secular ends-justifies-the-means ethic in a fear and power-toxic context. This clouded judgment and compromised the outcome. A more prudent Christian ethic such as Niebuhr's might have avoided the whole war.

The same moral risk of bad outcomes may apply to the refugee question.

A superior ethic can be derived from many biblical contexts. One, for example, is the Good Samaritan parable. Most Christians would have no trouble incorporating its lessons into their personal ethics. But it seems doubtful that all Christians agree on how this should or can be applied to moral dimensions of national policy. Jesus' parables should be understood in the context of Jesus' sacrificial life and death so that all peoples could become eligible to be members of the Kingdom of God. A grateful Christian response to this gift of grace is to, in Jesus words, "Go and do likewise"—like the Samaritan. Such fruits are what Jesus and his followers are known by.

But I have yet to hear or read Jesus quoted to support exclusion of refugees. Instead, the implicit argument against Muslims is guilt by association with ISIL in the word "Islam."

On this basis presidential candidates have likened Muslims to dogs, some rabid. We should accept only Christian Arabs. There should be special IDs, watch lists, and Mosque surveillance. We should carpet bomb the Caliphate into oblivion. None of the eight or more anti-Muslim letters in the Dispatch in recent weeks made a clear distinction between radicalized terrorists and peace-loving Muslims who reject ISIL's claim to be authentic Islam. This tactic places all Muslims in one scapegoat basket, which plays right into ISIL's effective propaganda recruitment and radicalization narrative.

The question before the US is still the same as it was for the Priest, Levite, and Samaritan in the parable: What is the right thing to do? Christians are not welcome as Christians in the Caliphate. Therefore one way to distinguish Christian morality from ISIL ideology is to not similarly stereotype all Muslims as potential sadistic terrorists. Nondiscrimination policies and allowing thoroughly vetted refugees sanctuary would demonstrate this moral difference from ISIL. These policies also work better for our internal national security than marginalizing and humiliating Muslims.

In his book, Ethics, Dietrich Bonhoeffer noted that Christianity in Germany in the 1930s often made the gospel merely a call to convert adulterers and drunkards, unable to inspire moral courage in good people to do the right thing. Jesus said many times, "Fear not!" Fear and fear mongering discourages risk-taking moral courage to act at the highest moral level.

I believe there is a redemptive opportunity in reaching out to the millions of peace-loving Muslims in the US and the world, and in doing all we can in allowing well-vetted refugees into our country.

(BD–12/14/15)

G–4 Up Close Christian Compassion

I take exception to the March 7 letter's undocumented assertion that the "secular and religious left . . . think that American Christians who argue against welcoming Syrian refugees are hateful, bigoted hypocrites." In the last three years, I wrote six pieces in support of welcoming as many well-vetted Syrian refugees as possible, and never implied such judgments. I claim simply to have a different interpretation of biblical morality.

Claims that the U.S. is "the most generous, compassionate nation on earth" are valid only because we are the richest and one of the largest nations on earth. My google inquiry disclosed that on a per capita basis, in the last decade Germany, France, the UK and Canada have averaged over 1.5 times as much foreign aid as the US and took in three times as many refugees - many more times this if only Syrians are counted. More significantly, this reality is the context of what the letter-writer correctly notes as the root cause: "leaders who have failed in their God-ordained duties." The chief of these failures was the US led coalition in the unjustified pre-emptive invasion of Iraq that set off the "Arab Spring," including the anti-Assad uprising in Syria and the spawning of ISIS.

Jesus said, "Love your enemies." Paul wrote to the Romans, "If your enemy is hungry, feed him." Taking such texts literally is only for starters. Christians are called to be "salt" in nudging governments toward peace, taking care not over-glorify their past while confessing national missteps. Christians are also called to non-violent courage, ready to suffer "for righteousness sake"—and to never cause suffering.

Almost all terrorists who caused deaths in the U.S. since 9–11 were radicalized in the US. For this, walls, bans, and "compassion-from-afar" are of no help. Better prevention is practicing Christian up-close compassion.

(BD–3/12/17)

G-7 Lost Children

In July 2014 the Dispatch published an opinion I wrote regarding the child refugee crisis at our Mexican border. This was in response to a syndicated columnist's opinion blaming the Obama administration, claiming we should instead "abide by the Constitution." In fact, some special provisions regarding children had been put in place by the Bush administration.

In January 2015 a letter of mine was published in the Dispatch that briefly reviewed how the New Pathways program (NP) had been helping rehabilitate homeless families with children in the Brainerd area. I had been on the NP board and I encouraged anyone interested to join. Because of cutbacks in government funding, that program's future is now doubt. The NP program and border issue are similar in that both involve homeless families.

Now the Trump administration has seemingly taken matters to a new morality low. Attorney General Jeff Sessions earlier announced that families with children seeking refugee status would have their children taken from them. Then General Kelly remarked that this should serve as a "strong deterrent." But as I pointed out in my previous piece, in some of these countries, young girls live in constant fear of being raped, and boys are warned they will be shot if they refuse to join a gang.

New reports estimate that there are now 1,500 immigrant children placed in foster care that are not accounted for. Former Republican Sen. Rick Santorum glibly said their parents should be more responsible. But perhaps some parents may feel losing their sobbing child at the border is best of all options. A spokesperson remarked that the government wasn't legally responsible once there was foster care placement. For the Trump administration, everything seemingly has become what is declared legal, discarding any overarching moral dimension such as the Bible brings to all human relationships.

(BD—5/31/18)

H. Political

H–1 Positive Partisanship

It is not unusual for writers on political issues, from syndicated columnists to occasional letter writers, to quote a founding father to support a partisan position. However, such citations seldom represent the whole truth because then as now, there was usually someone with an opposing view, and the outcome was usually a compromise. It is important, therefore, to have some insight into the intrinsic nature of political partisanship in realistically reaching solutions to modern problems. The Jefferson—Hamilton relationship is one example, well-documented in the recent book, *Thomas Jefferson,* by Jon Meacham.

Jefferson is best known as the author of the Declaration of Independence, but he was also a major figure in what evolved in the next four decades. He received a classical education at William and Mary College, and before 1776 he was in the House of Burgesses and Governor of the Commonwealth of Virginia. He served as Ambassador to France and Secretary of State in President Washington's cabinet. This was followed by a term as Vice President to John Adams before he served two terms as President of the United States.

Jefferson, along with many other leaders expressed hope that the level of unity experienced in achieving independence from England would continue into the early years of self-government. But this was not to be. Jefferson was a rural Virginian and early on found himself at odds with Alexander Hamilton, a New Yorker and Columbia graduate who was Secretary of the Treasury for Washington at the same time as Jefferson was Secretary of State. Although oversimplified, there is considerable truth in stating that the differences between these two men represent the major political divide in our history down to the present.

The political party of Jefferson was called Republican, although it has no historical or ideological connection with the present Republican Party, which had its origins in Abraham Lincoln. The word "republican" then meant broad suffrage (voting rights) with relatively short office terms between elections. Hamilton's Party was called "Federalist," after the Federalist Papers he helped write to persuade the colonies to ratify the Constitution. He was from New York, married into a wealthy family. The difference thus became a rural farming southerner vs. an urban northerner who was focused more on manufacturing, marketing, and financial institutions.

Jefferson's political ideas came mostly from the English Enlightenment philosopher John Locke whose basic principles were equal rights of all people governed by a "consent" or social contract constitution in which citizens agree to give up some rights to secure those most important, agreeing to accept majority votes of elected representatives. Hamilton's stance came mostly from another British philosopher, Thomas Hobbes, who saw mostly the selfish and confrontational nature of most humans who need a strong Federal government run by those most gifted to govern. He was skeptical that enough good governing candidates could come from broad suffrage. Therefore Hamilton favored long terms for the executive and one legislative branch of government. He even suggested that the English monarchical system with a king might be considered. Jefferson had a strong distrust in such ideas, especially when they were linked with financial interests exerted as political power.

The Jefferson vs. Hamilton differences still exist in the current Democratic and Republican parties respectively, but with some differences that will not be enumerated here. The main reason for noting these differences is described in the following quotation from Jefferson at the start of his first term as President: "Nothing shall be spared on my part to obliterate traces of party and consolidate the nation." (Meacham, 2012). Three years later he said this attempt "was honorably pursued for a year or two and spurned by them." The best he could hope for "was a truce between himself and his opponents, not a permanent peace." He decided political divisions were intrinsic—what mattered most was how they were managed effectively. Parties are a check on one another.

While he was President years before, Washington spoke to this issue in a letter to Jefferson: "How unfortunate it is that internal dissensions should be harrowing . . . I believe it will be difficult, if not impossible to manage the reins of government or to keep the parts of it together; for if, instead of laying our shoulders to the machine after measures are decided upon, one pulls this way and another that before utility of the thing is fully tried, it must inevitably be torn asunder . . . lost, perhaps forever."

During their entire political careers, Jefferson and Hamilton stood staunchly against each other's political philosophy. But they respected each other and worked out compromise stances. Jefferson did not try to make Federalist Adam's presidency fail and Hamilton did not attempt to make Jefferson's presidency fail. Jefferson even kept a bust of Hamilton in his home in retirement.

I see important relevance of this history to our national politics of extreme negativism today. Parties seemingly cannot find anything positive in one another and will resort by whatever means possible to stop legislation or appointments, shut down the government, and even default on the nation's debt. Legislation that has no chance of being approved by other branches is meaninglessly passed and attempts to kill a bill or repeal a law are not accompanied by a credible positive alternative. A constant drumbeat of negative criticism echoed by the media erodes confidence and trust in our federal government. A suspicion develops that all this is a coordinated strategy to make a presidency fail.

My view is that when any presidency fails, we all suffer no matter what the reason and which party holds the office. A deliberate attempt to make a presidency fail based only on ideology or imperfect performance is an exercise of shooting ourselves in the foot - or worse. We would do well to look to the political practices of Washington, Jefferson, and Hamilton to get ourselves out of the partisan gridlock we are in. These men would likely admonish us that "Partisanship is a permanent reality. Accept this fact, get on with it, and work together, or you may permanently harm the Republic."

(BD–1/5/14)

H-2 Biblical Justice

Tea party members and some of our Minnesota politicians claim to be practicing Christians. I would like them to explain how this virtue relates to socio-economic justice because the Bible has hundreds of times more words on this subject than about the few sexuality issues that get so much attention.

To illustrate, the Exodus was redemption of a select people from economic bondage by a powerful minority. The subsequent trek of this freed group toward a promised land has been characterized as a "journey toward the common good," with Mount Sinai a pause to get the moral rules for a just society. Although largely achieved under King David, their descendants became corrupted by affluence, and the kingdom split. Because of false confidence in military power, fraud in the market place, and ostentatious wealth that disregarded vulnerable widows, orphans, and refugees, the prophets predicted their demise or captivity.

Jesus had nothing good to say about the super-wealthy, he repeatedly warned of the dangers of riches, and he showed special concern for the vulnerable poor. The Bible says nothing against government or taxes per se, but it has a lot to say against persons who become unjustly rich through tax systems and governments not committed to ethically fair distribution of wealth. Disproportionately more is expected of those with much. The wider the gap between rich and poor, the poorer is the health and longevity of any society.

Measured by these biblical standards, in multiple ways we have been going the wrong direction in the last decade. Whether recognized or not, we have been led toward practicing Ayn Rand's "Virtue of selfishness" philosophy. Candidates who claim to be Christian should be expected to relate their political stances on issues to the Bible.

(BD—8/5/11)

I. Economic

I-1 Biblical Economics

Earlier this year Pope Francis made a stir when he said the Catholic Church was too obsessed with certain sexuality issues. This month he seems to have topped this with his official apostolic statement, *Evanglii Gaudium*, which was mostly a warning against the idolatry of money. He cited evils of "unfettered capitalism," and "trickle-down" theory, which was not an attack of capitalism per se. But Rush Limbaugh slammed back calling his official statement, "Pure Marxism." The Pope is to be commended for speaking against the practices that can increase wealth disparity to dangerous tipping points.

Numerous U.S. statistics document marked increase in U.S. wealth disparity over the last 50 years. Since 1980, the top 1% have increased their share of the income by an astounding $1.1 trillion. The average net worth of the top 10% doubled from $2 million to $4 million, whereas the bottom 75% remained well below $100,000. Five percent of the population now has over 60% of the nation's private wealth. Meanwhile, a fulltime wage was 11% lower in 2004 than in 1973, adjusted for inflation, even though productivity increased by 78%. Compared to other developed countries, only Mexico, Brazil and South Africa have greater wealth disparity than the U.S. Facilitated by big money lobbying, more and more laws have been passed that help the rich at the expense of the poor.

Interpreting this trend, one analysis concluded: "Extreme wealth and disparity are reaching levels never before seen and are getting worse . . . Extreme wealth and disparity is economically inefficient . . . politically corrosive. . .socially divisive. . .environmentally destructive. . .unethical. . .and not inevitable."

An opposing argument is that inequality is necessary for a capitalistic system: "Without the wealth creators there can be no long-term prosperity." "Without the wealthy there would be few jobs." "Without greed we have bad cars. . . " There is some truth in these assertions, but they imply that there is no extreme of disparity that is harmful and the more disparity the better. This assumption has been challenged. One study comparing countries with extreme vs. moderate disparity found the extreme group to have worse statistics in life expectancy, mental illness, teenage pregnancy rates, violence, imprisonment, and potential social mobility.

The above judgments are from secular sources. Since the Bible is frequently cited for sexual aberrations that allegedly seriously threaten our future, the Bible should also be examined for wealth disparity concerns. Deuteronomy admonishes compassion for the sojourner and widows, along with a vision that "There shall be no poor among you." Market place fraud (then false balances and measures) is condemned, and universal debt release every seven years was urged to limit excessive wealth disparity. The biblical record links the prosperity under David and Solomon to moral laxity and fracture of the country into two nation-states.

Some generations later, the prophets warned both Israel and Judah about odious wealth at the expense of the poor: "Woe to you who are complacent in

Zion, you lie of beds inlaid with ivory. . .you who trample upon the needy . . . and bring the poor of the land to their end." The only sexual sin they cited was marital adultery. Also, "I hate, I despise your religious feasts; I cannot stand your holy assemblies . . . But let justice roll down like a river, righteousness like a never-failing stream!" The predicted judgments of the prophets against both Israel and Judah came at the hands of "pagan" foreign powers that were described as God's unwitting temporary servants.

Jesus described himself as being in the line of these prophets, and his message at the outset was "Blessed are you poor . . . Woe to you who are rich. . . " This was not just a warning about eternal welfare but to the temporal risk individuals and societies take on with excessive wealth disparity. Greed displaces compassion— "Where your treasure is, there your heart will be also." Disciples are called to be God's stewards, not selfish owners. "To whom much is given, much is expected . . . Even as you did this to the least of these my (poor) brethren, you did it unto me . . . Woe to you . . . hypocrites, for you tithe mint, dill, and cumin but neglect the weightier matters of the law, justice, mercy, and faith." The books of Daniel and Revelation cite the most powerful nations in history as being the most vulnerable to becoming "beasts" that slip into economic injustices that are both signs and causes of their eventual undoing.

The above secular and biblical analyses of wealth disparities are consistent with each other. Multiple prominent theologians over the last sixty years have written about the biblical relevance to U.S. culture. Two examples will be cited: "We might ask to what extent Amos' indictment of society is applicable to us today . . . it is fully applicable. It takes no skill to point out that our society, like that of ancient Israel, is shot through with that which Amos denounced; injustice and greed, pleasure-loving ease, and venality. The indictment of Amos is an indictment of all societies, including our own" (John Bright, "The Kingdom of God," 1953); "The lines from Jeremiah well characterize the aggressive acquisitiveness that has marked the US economy for a generation with a shameless greed at the expense of the neighbor" (Walter Brueggemann, "Journey to the Common Good," 2010). When a sector of secular wisdom corresponds with biblical wisdom, it may be significant.

In sheer numbers, the Bible has hundreds of times more verses related to moral money/material matters than to sexual issues, especially if only the usual big three of our time are considered (birth control, abortion, and same-sex relationships). This fact alone warrants proper balance, especially if sexual priorities become rationalization for ignoring broader biblical precepts.

Just as in the time of Jesus and the prophets, biblical economic morality may be muted in our culture because of the power of money that may be withheld from volunteer organizations and small businesses with leaders who speak out against greed. But even though authentic prophetic messages have never been popular, such theological warnings are out there today. There may be significant risk in not listening. (BD–12/7/13)

I–3 The Cliffs: Fiscal, Tyrannical, or Integrity?

The Jan. 3 Brainerd Dispatch published a guest opinion by Robert Ringer about what he regards as the nation's next "cliff," which he thinks will be much worse than the fiscal cliff that he thinks we had long ago. This next cliff is a government tyranny cliff. He defines this as "Americans losing their freedoms because of the "government's evermore (increasing) control over our personal lives through increasing taxes and regulations."

A point Ringer made on which there is quite universal agreement is that our government is not working as well as it should in solving our problems, but the author seems to display one of the reasons for our difficulties more than make the negative judgments of others stick.

A clearer understanding of Robert Ringer's political philosophy is available from his web site where he posts interviews he has done with various politicians and authors. He currently has the co-authors of a book titled, "Free Market Revolution—How Ayn Rand's Ideas Can End Big Government." Ringer's approach seems consistent with the "Objectivism" political and economic philosophy of Ayn Rand. I know of one former Wall Street business man now running his own investment counseling business who published an article titled "Ayn Rand: The Goddess of the Great Recession" (meaning that starting in 2008). One of her chief admirers was Allen Greenspan, who seems to have fallen from grace but his self-acknowledged intellectual mentor's ideas are still alive and well.

Rand has been likened to Karl Marx in that "both were self-proclaimed prophets who both denied the existence of a loving God." Both also preach a route to utopia. A Rand admirer who faced some criticism for pushing Rand's philosophy was US House Representative Paul Ryan. As a Roman Catholic, some Catholic groups called him to task not only his promotion of Rand, but also for incorporating her stance into his budget proposal because of the way it would decimate the poor with cuts to Food Stamps and Medicaid. Ryan then somewhat distanced himself from Rand but he has not yet changed his proposed bill. Rand's philosophy is best expounded in her novel, "Atlas Shrugged."

Rand's philosophy built on the "virtue of selfishness" to achieve power and wealth is not hard to sell. The problem is that "Power corrupts and absolute power corrupts absolutely." Such philosophies can lead to lead to anti-democratic anarchies, oligarchies, or dictatorships. Abraham Lincoln once said, "Most men can stand adversity, but if you want to test a man's character, give him power. That is why the U/S/ Constitution is based on balances of power. To do this effectively requires a constant effort to maintain high standards of integrity for all involved.

(BD-1/8/13)

I-7 Tax Return Transparency

President Trump's tax returns are still in the news, both nationally and locally. Many reports neglect serious considerations regarding legality vs. morality, and the risks of non-transparency.

One argument justifying the President's refusal to release his returns is that it is legal to keep tax returns confidential, which is true. It would be legal for me to refuse to give copies to a mortgage company from whom I was once seeking a mortgage. But then it would also have been legal for the company to refuse to give me a mortgage. It makes good business sense. Disclosure reduces risk.

There is a difference between what is legal and what is moral, which President Trump seems to not recognize. The moral bar is higher. Slavery was once legal in the U.S., but many judged the U.S slave system to be immoral, and laws were changed accordingly, at great cost. Laws can be passed with dubious unintended consequences, if not intent. It is always safer to try to act by a moral rather than just a legal code.

One of the major risks of non-transparency is that if President Trump has something significant to hide, operating with anxiety that it will come to light could seriously compromise emotional stability and judgment - a sort of self-blackmail. This seemed quite obvious to many, and there is little the President has done since in office to erase a suspicion that he is hiding something significant.

The reality is that the entire nation is now at risk. After all, President Trump's denials and reassurances, if something serious comes to light, it could be one of the most blatant presidential betrayals of supporter trust in history. Time will likely tell. We now can only hope we get through it with minimal damage.

(BD-5/26/17)

J. Foreign Policy

J–2 Iran Nuclear Risks

I must take some exception to the letter that claims a treaty with Iran will increase the threat of nuclear war more than a failed attempt would. The opposite argument deserves attention.

This treaty effort is not just an Obama-Kerry thing. All four of the other UN Security Council members (England, France, Russia, China) plus Germany are part of the negotiations. If a treaty now fails, both Israel and he U.S. may be seriously alienated from some of these countries.

The anti-treaty argument is that there should be tougher sanctions coordinated by the six nations and U.N. may come apart without a treaty, especially since he congressional majority preemptively stuck their finger in the eye of every coalition member. Sanctions could end up far less stringent.

If the treaty fails, Russia and possibly China could side with Iran against Israel, which could put the U.S. against Russia on this issue. This would not bode well.

In September 2002, Netanyahu testified before a U.S. House hearing that "There is no question that Saddam is working on producing an atomic weapon. . .I can guarantee you that removing have positive effects on the region." These assessments were wrong. Do we want to risk following his lead again?

To promote a holy war after we killed over 100,000 Muslims to bring down Saddam is a dubious morality. Saddam not only had been an effective deterrent to Iran's ambitions, but his removal spawned ISIS, making things worse for regional Christians, not better.

I don't claim certainty for either side of the argument. But I think a 10-year "breathing space" to test Iran's commitment under the close watch of inspectors is less risky than the risks without a treaty.

(BD–2/23/15)

J–3 God's Foreign Policy?

A recent letter claims the U.S should support God's foreign policy—an undivided state of Israel against our common enemy, Islam-based terrorism. In asserting that God protects those who unconditionally support Israel, the letter supports dangerously violent religious fundamentalism.

The writer erroneously assumes the Old Testament covenant promises to Abraham's descendants are unconditional. However, the repeated admonitions about God's blessings vs. curses are prefaced with, "If you. . ." do, or do not, obey. The prophets predicted God's judgment for the failures of Israel and Judah to "do justice." Subsequently, Assyria and Babylon devastated both Jewish states. According to the Bible, these nations did this unknowingly as God's temporary "servants" of judgment. Thus, in God's view, no nations are unconditionally "untouchable."

The letter totally ignores the new covenant under which Jesus told Pilate, "My kingship is not of this world; if it were, my servants would fight to prevent my arrest." The unjust crucifixion of Jesus was done through cooperation of religious and political persons in power. Part of what is "new" in the new covenant is that Golgatha signifies the end of God-sanctioned political violence. Thus Jesus' "kingship-messiahship" disappointed most of his contemporaries.

God's faithful servants are to work for peace and justice for all people, primarily through persuasion and example. They accept the need of protective police power to insure justice, especially freedom of speech and religion. But they are not to invoke God to justify a violent "fight," citing religious differences. This fundamentalism risks God's judgment in history from the God who controls nature and history.

Politicized religion is usually based on selective, proof-texting of sacred writings rather than sound, holistic, interpretation. One should always be wary of any foreign policy stance that claims no doubt about whose side God is on.

(BD–12/10/11)

Bibliography

Ahlstrom, Sydney E. *A Religious History of the American People.* New Haven: Yale University Press, 1972

Annals of Internal Medicine, Firearm Injury Prevention, (1 Feb, 1998)

Annals of Internal Medicine, Reducing Firearm- Related Injury and Death, (7 April, 2015)

Barth, Karl. *Dogmatics in Outline.* New York: Harper and Row, 1959

Bonhoeffer, Dietrich. *Ethics.* New York: Macmillan, 1948

———. *The Cost of Discipleship.* New York: Macmillan, 1948

Borg, Marcus. *Convictions.* New York: Harper Collins, 2014

Bright, John. *The Kingdom of God.* Nashville: Abington, 1953

Brooks, David. *New York Times* editorial, (June 2, 2017)

Bruggemann, Walter. *The Journey to the Common Good.* New York: Westminster John Knox, 2010

Campolo, Tony, and Shane Claiborne "The Evangelicalism of Old White Men is Dead." *New York Times* editorial. November 29, 2016

Caplan, Arthur. *When Medicine Went Mad.* Totowa: Humana Press, 1992

Dowland, Seth. "The Politics of Whiteness." *The Christian Century* (July 4, 2018) 26–31

Erdahl, Lowell O. *Pro-Life, Pro-Peace.* Minneapolis: Augsburg, 1986

Evangelical Lutheran Church in America. *Evangelical Lutheran Worship.* Minneapolis: Augsburg Fortress, 2006

Fea, John, "The Fear Sweepstakes." The *Christian Century* 14 (July 4, 2018) 22-25.

Forde, Gerhard. *On Being a Theologian of the Cross.* Grand Rapids: Wm. B. Eerdmans, 1997

Fosdick, Harry Emerson. *Putting Christ into Uniform.* Sermon preached at Riverside Church, New York City, Nov. 12, 1939, and published by the church in pamphlet form. Reference from Erdahl, Lowell O. *Pro-Life, Pro-Peace.* Minneapolis: Augsburg, 1986

Fretheim, Terrence. *God and World in the Old Testament.* Nashville: Abington, 2005.

Friedman, R.C., and R.I. Downy. "Homosexuality." *New Eng J Med* 331(1994) 924

Hall, Douglas J. *The Cross in Our Context.* Minneapolis: Fortress, 2003

———. *The Steward, a biblical symbol come of age.* Eugene: Wipf and Stock, 1990

Harnack, Adolph von, *What is Christianity?* Translated by Thomas Baily Sanders. Library of Religion and Culture. New York: Harper and Brothers, 1957, 69–70. This paragraph was cited by Leander E. Keck in *Who is Jesus?* Edinburgh: T&T Clark, University of South Carolina, 2010

Heim, David. "Public Witness and How it is Compromised." The *Christian Century* 14 (July 4, 2018) 3.

Johnson, William Stacy. *A Time to Embrace*. Grand Rapids: Eerdmans, 2006

Kierkegaard, Soren. *Fear and Trembling*. Princeton University Press, 1941

———. *For Self-Examination*. Minneapolis: Augsburg, 1950.

———. *Works of Love*. New York: Harper and Row, 1962

The Koran, New York, Penguin Books, 1999

Krajeski, J. *Textbook of Homosexuality and Mental Health*. Cabaj and Stein, eds, Washington, DC: American Psychiatric Press, 1996

Limburg, James. *The Prophets and the Powerless*. Lima: First Academic Press Edition, 2001

"Marshall Plan Speech." www.marshallfoundation.org/.../marshall-plan-speech

Marty, Peter. "Hollowed Out by Fear." The *Christian Century* 14, (July 4, 2018) 3

Meacham, *Thomas Jefferson: The Art of Power*. New York: Random House, 2012

Meeks, M. Douglas. *The Doctrine of God and Political Economy*. Minneapolis: Fortress, 2000.

Minneapolis Star Tribune, opinion letter, Feb. 8, 2017

Moore, Gary. "Ayn Rand, Goddess of the Great Recession." *Christianity Today* (September 2010), 37–40

———. "Goddess of Meanness and Greed: Ayn Rand and the Religious Right." *Word and World*, edited by Fred Gaiser, Luther Seminary, St. Paul. Supplement Series 6. October 2010. 21–31

Niebuhr, Reinhold. *Beyond Tragedy*. New York: Charles Scribner's Sons, 1937

———. *Moral Man and Immoral Society*. New York: Charles Scribner's, 1932

Peterson, Charles R. "Science and Scripture." *Lutheran Forum* 27 (1993) 48–51

Putnam, Robert, and David E. Campbell, *American Grace: How Religion Divides and Unites Us*. New York: Simon and Schuster, 2010

Rand, Ayn. *Atlas Shrugged*. New York: Penguin, 1957

Rasmussen, Larry. *Earth Honoring Faith*. New York: Oxford University Press, 2013

Reed, Ralph. "Conservative Coalition Holds Together." *Wall Street Journal* (February 13, 1995) A-14

Reid, T. R. *The Healing of America*. New York: The Penguin Press, 2009

Relman, Arnold S. *A Second Opinion*, Cambridge: The Century Foundation, 2007 The Arrow material summarized by Relman is: Arrow, Kenneth J. "Uncertainty and the Welfare Economics of Medical Care." *American Economics Review*. (1963) 53: 941–973

Robertson, Pat. *The New Millennium*. Franklin TN Publishing Group, 1990

Snyder, Lois (Staff Editor/Author) *Ethics Manual, Sixth Edition*, American College of Physicians, Reprinted from *Annals of Internal Medicine*, 3 January 2012.

Suchokie, Marjorie Hewitt. *The Fall to Violence*. New York: The Continuum, 1994

Tillich, Paul. "We Live in Two orders" in *The Shaking of the Foundations*. New York: Charles Scribner's Sons, 1948

Time Magazine, feature article on Karl Barth, May 31, 1963

Wall Street Journal editorial. "Greed is Good." (February 7, 2009) W1. This quotation and source are from Moore, *Word and World*.

Index of Names

Index of Subjects

Index of Annotated Scripture References

Proverbs

9:10, 119, The fear of the Lord is the beginning of wisdom.

14:34, 117, Righteousness exalts a nation, but sin is a reproach to its people.

Isaiah

5:8–10, 26, "Woe to those who build house to house" (odious materialism).

6:1–13, 117, God said, "Whom shall I send?" I said, "Here I am! Send me."

10:1–2, 26, 28, Woe to those who deny justice to the needy.

10:5, 26, 28, "Ah, Assyria, the rod of my anger, the staff of my fury."

10:21, 40, A remnant will return.

11:1–3;, 120, Prediction of a messiah who manifests fear of God.

31:1, 24, Beware of false trust in horses and chariots of national power.

40:1–8, 40, Iniquity pardoned; a way prepared for return; a gentle messiah.

40:7, 42, The grass withers, flowers fade, but God's word stands forever.

43:1, 108, "Fear not, for I have redeemed you; I have called you by name."

53: 1–12, 23, 40 , Prediction of a suffering-servant messiah.

58:3–5, 24, Your fasting is to "hit with a wicked fist." My fast is to be humble.

59:14, 26, "Justice is turned back . . . Truth has fallen in the public square."

Jeremiah

2:34–35, 28, On your skirts is the life-blood of the innocent poor.

5:7–8, 29, How can I pardon their adultery and harlotry?

5:28, 27–28 , They became rich but wicked toward the needy.

5:30–31, 27, The prophets prophesy falsely: an appalling thing!

7:8–11, 27, Will you steal then come to my house as a den for robbers?

8:22, 27, "Is there no balm in Gilead?" (to help the sin–sick souls?).

22:3, 28, 81, Do justice rather than violence to the alien.

31:31–34, 97, God's covenant was broken.

Ezekiel

22:6–7, 29, "The sojourner suffers extortion in your midst."

22:11, 29, "One commits abomination with his neighbor's wife."

Hosea

10:13–14, 24, Trusting primarily in strong warriors is a weak strategy.

12:7–8, 26, Wealth from false balances will not offset the consequences.

Amos

4:1–5, 25, God dislikes oppression of the poor and needy.

5:10–12, 27, Justice will come against those who practice injustice.

6:4–7, 26, Woe to those who lie upon beds of ivory.

8:4–5, 25, 27, God will not forget those who use false balances.